CHEVROLET
PICKUPS

MIKE MUELLER

MOTORBOOKS
INTERNATIONAL

On the front cover:
As in 1936 and 1947, Chevrolet began the 1955 model year with a "leftover" first-series model (left) then introduced a brand new second-series truck midyear.

On the frontispiece:
The nose of one of Chevrolet's earliest trucks, a 1920 model.

On the title page:
This 1954 Chevy 3100 is the last of the Advance Design trucks.

On the back cover, left: Chevrolet actually started selling trucks to civilians before World War II ended, as part of a plan to keep vital American businesses solvent. **Right:** Introduced in 1918, the Model 490 half-ton truck was based on the low-cost Chevrolet automobile of the same name and sold sans bodywork. Custom wooden cabs, like the one on this 1918 half-ton, were either built by the buyer or purchased from an aftermarket supplier.

Printed in Hong Kong

CONTENTS

	Acknowledgments	7
	Introduction: *80 Years and Counting*	9
CHAPTER 1	**Bow-Tie Beginnings:** *Chevrolet Trucks Debut in 1918*	17
CHAPTER 2	**Real Steel:** *True Chevy Pickups Emerge*	35
CHAPTER 3	**First In Peace:** *The Advance-Design Years: 1947–1955*	57
CHAPTER 4	**Thoroughly Modern:** *Task-Force Trucks, 1955–1959*	73
CHAPTER 5	**A Star is Born:** *Carried Away by Cameo*	89
CHAPTER 6	**When Car Met Truck:** *The El Camino Hits the Road*	103
CHAPTER 7	**Sixties Sensations:** *All-New Trucks for an All-New Decade*	119
CHAPTER 8	**Putting The Driver First:** *Corvair 95 Pickups, 1961–1964*	133
CHAPTER 9	**Still Crazy After All Those Years:** *Chevy Trucks Roll into the Seventies*	143
CHAPTER 10	**Epilogue:** *Chevy Pickups Just Keep on Truckin'*	157
	Index	168

Acknowledgments

This project initially began more than two years before these words were keystroked, leaving this humble author little choice but to extend endless amounts of gratitude to all the wonderfully kind, cooperative and forgiving folk who showed so much patience with me along the way. First and foremost is my much-too-kind editor at Motorbooks, Lee Klancher, who took all the abuse from above up in Minnesota while I missed deadline after deadline down here in Kennesaw, Georgia. Second in line (but first in my heart) are my wife Joyce and her three kids, Chelsea, Lucy and Henry. You guys sure put up with a lotta guff while I was so busy missing all those deadlines—don't worry, though, you'll get yours. My best friend (and brother) Dave Mueller, in Flatville,

The author's wife, Joyce Mueller, puts a Chevrolet pickup to work in 1998 delivering a load of Girl Scout cookies with her daughters, Lucy (left) and Chelsea.

Illinois, was also there when I needed him every time, as were my other best friends (and not my brothers) Bill Tower, of Plant City, Florida, and Ray Quinlan, in Champaign, Illinois. Don't let me forget my sister, Kathy Young, and her husband Frank (definitely not my best friend), also of Champaign. Where would I be if Kathy and Frank (and their kids, Michelle and Jason) hadn't taken me into their fabulous home time and time again during my many photo junkets across the country? Probably in the gutter.

Many other people—homeowners, truck collectors, restoration experts, enthusiasts, club officers, etc.—also helped so much, both by locating the beautiful vintage Chevy pickups you see here and by allowing me on their property to photograph said trucks. But there just isn't room here to list everyone. You know who you are, as do I. And I won't forget.

Archival research material came from many sources, all of whom I'll forever speak highly of in a crowd: Mark Patrick at the Detroit Public Library in the Motor City, Kim Miller at the AACA Library and Research Center in Hershey, Pennsylvania; Larry Scheef and his wonderful staff at the American Truck Historical Society, now relocated to Kansas City, Missouri; fellow automotive historian Bob Ackerson in Schenevus, New York; and Dave Newell's Chevrobilia in Orinda, California. I just couldn't lose with these people behind me.

Vintage literature and brochures were supplied by ever-present dealer/collector Walter Miller in Syracuse, New York; Bob Johnson's Auto Literature in Farmingham, Massachussetts; and Dan Bower's Factory Automanuals in Flint, Michigan. Also of great assistance in this vein was the late George Reed, who sadly passed away in May 2001. I was greatly impressed with George's vast knowledge during the short time I knew him, and he too never once failed to help out when I came demanding. He will be missed, both personally and professionally.

Loads of thanks also go to all the men and women who allowed me to photograph their fine pickups for this book. They are, in basic order of appearance: 1955 Chevrolet 3100 (green); Ken Craig, Lakeland, Florida; 1953 Ford F-100, Carl Lane, Lakeland, Florida; 1951 Chevrolet one-ton & 1952 Ford tractor, Wayne Alderson, Independence, Missouri; 1950 Chevrolet COE & 1959 Chevrolet El Camino, Bill Smith, Hershey, Pennsylvania; 1957 Chevrolet 150 sedan & 1957 Chevrolet Cameo (black), Steve Tate, Liberty, Missouri; 1961 Chevrolet Corvair 95 Rampside, Dave Hanks, Peoria, Illinois; 1963 Chevrolet Corvair 95 Rampside, L.C. Smith, Hanna City, Illinois; 1967 Chevrolet CST, Chris Short, Port St. John, Florida; 1918 Chevrolet Model 490, Tom Snivley, Bryan, Ohio; 1920 Chevrolet Model T, Everett & Carol Nebergall, Helena, Ohio; 1927 Chevrolet one-ton, Dana Corporation, Toledo, Ohio; 1932 Chevrolet, Jim Benjaminson, Walhalla, North Dakota; 1930 Chevrolet roadster, Dar Pace, Coral Gables, Florida; 1936 Chevrolet, Russ Berg, Jr., Grand Haven, Michigan; 1937 Chevrolet, Don & Shirley Ulrich, Muncie, Indiana; 1940 Chevrolet, Richard Walters, Fremont, Ohio; 1937 Diamond T Model 80, Del DeYoung, Friesland, Wisconsin; 1935 Chevrolet Suburban, Walter & Penny Deck, Ridge Farm, Illinois; 1957 GMC Suburban, Ralph Westcott, Largo, Florida; 1954 Chevrolet 3100, Rudy Radke, Fargo, North Dakota; 1949 Chevrolet 3100, Bill Hayes, Sr., Lemont, Illinois; 1953 Chevrolet 3100, Ken Craig, Lakeland, Florida; 1955 Chevrolet 3100 "first-series" (black), Rich New, Adairsville, Georgia; 1947 Chevrolet "first-series" 5th-wheel "dualie," Steve Tate, Liberty, Missouri; 1955 Chevrolet 3100 (red); Rich New, Adairsville, Georgia; 1955 Chevrolet Bel Air convertible, Bruce & Linda Finley, Lakeland, Florida; 1948 Ford F-1, Sam Smith, Adairsville, Georgia; 1957 Chevrolet 3200, Terry Adreon, Bloomington, Illinois;

1956 Chevrolet 3100 & 1959 Chevrolet Fleetside Apache, Ronnie Larkins, High Point, North Carolina; 1959 Chevrolet 3100 Stepside (black), Eldon Taylor, Maysville, Missouri; 1959 Chevrolet 4x4, Lee Eidem, Glyndon, Minnesota; 1956 Chevrolet Cameo & 1958 Chevrolet Cameo, Ralph Peddicord, Westminster Maryland; 1955 Chevrolet Cameo, Ken Craig, Lakeland, Florida; 1957 Chevrolet Cameo, Jerry & Vickie Hanneken, Mt. Zion, Illinois; 1958 Chevrolet Cameo (black), Jake Andrews, Coshocton, Ohio; 1955 GMC Suburban Pickup, 1958 GMC Suburban Pickup & 1959 GMC Suburban Pickup, Ralph Westcott, Largo, Florida; 1964 Chevrolet El Camino & 1986 Chevrolet El Camino, Bill Smith, Hershey, Pennsylvania; 1970 Chevrolet El Camino SS 454, Robert Inhoff, Jeanette, Pennsylvania; 1981 Chevrolet El Camino Royal Knight, Daryl Miller, Normal, Illinois; 1979 Ford Ranchero, Gene Mackrancy, Port Vue, Pennsylvania; 1961 Chevrolet C-10, Ray Guin Charlotte, North Carolina; 1961 Chevrolet C-10 (deluxe two-tone), Paul Garlick, Iron Mountain, Michigan; 1963 Chevrolet C-10 Stepside, Tim Simmons, Gadsden, Alabama; 1965 Chevrolet C-10 Fleetside, Jerry Willimas, Altoona, Alabama; 1964 Chevrolet Corvair 95 Rampside & 1964 Chevrolet Corvair, Billy Bruce, Tyrone, Georgia; 1962 Chevrolet Corvan, Louie Prior, Indianapolis, Indiana; 1965 Chevrolet Greenbriar, Jean Allan, Southport, Indiana; 1968 Chevrolet C-10 Custom, Kendall Radke, Fargo, North Dakota; 1972 Chevrolet Super Cheyenne, Rob Granger, Eustis, Florida; 1973 Chevrolet C-10, Pete Woyen, Fargo, North Dakota; 1946 Chevrolet & 1990 Chevrolet SS 454, Jim Semon, Westlake, Ohio.

I hope your wait was worth it.

—Mike Mueller
April 2002

Introduction

80 Years and Counting

Chassis view of the Chevrolet One-Ton Truck showing the sturdy construction which insures maximum service and minimum wear. Chassis, $1325 f.o.b. Flint, Michigan.

Above
Like all early trucks, Chevrolet's first were sold in bare-chassis form—bodies were supplied by aftermarket suppliers. Shown here is a 1920 one-ton Model T. Both the big Model T and its Model 490 little brother were introduced in 1918.

Left
While Chevrolet did lead the truck market in sales throughout the 1950s, Ford was never far behind. The two rivals traded milestone introductions: Chevy had the first new postwar pickup in 1947, Ford then followed with its first F-series model in 1948. Dearborn's legendary F-100 (right) debuted in 1953; Chevrolet then trumped that with its new Task Force trucks in 1955.

It was a dynasty that dwarfed even the accomplishments of today's New York Yankees, a team that in November 2001 fell short of winning its fourth consecutive World Series in the bottom of the ninth inning of game seven. It was a stay in the top seat that made Franklin Roosevelt's four terms in the White House seem like an overnight visit—a dominance of its field that Bill Gates would envy.

"It" was Chevrolet's record-setting performance in truck sales. For 30 years—three decades—Chevys were America's best-selling trucks. From 1938 to 1967 nobody in this country sold more pickups, flatbeds, vans, buses, or big-rigs. Nobody, not even Ford, eclipsed Chevy during this period, though it came close a few times before finally reclaiming the crown from the reigning champs in 1968.

Detroit's two main rivals had traded the lead on various occasions in the 1920s and 1930s before Dearborn's visit to the top in 1937. Once in its soon-to-be customary spot atop the goods-hauling heap, Chevrolet proceeded to win sales battle after sales battle through one world war, one police action in Korea, and into one escalating military intervention in Southeast Asia. A dozen Yankee world championships, five presidents, and one baby boom later, Ford managed to bring an end to Chevy's winning streak. Today the Blue-Oval band is on a similar run and probably will break the Bow-Tie boys' record shortly, considering that Chevrolet's three-decade stretch technically skipped a few years during World War II."

Ford promotional people these days are nonchalant when touting their quarter-century of truck sales leadership. They also seemingly take it for granted that everyone now knows which century-old car company both originated the Big Three truck race in 1917 *and* introduced Americans to their first factory-complete, all-steel, half-ton pickup eight years later. Sure, Ford was first, but Chevrolet showed the world the right way to sell pickups, again and again. As far as the light-truck market was concerned from the 1930s to the 1970s, the more things changed, the more they stayed the same.

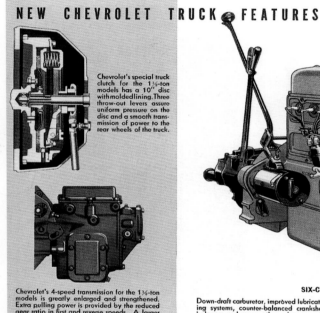

NEW CHEVROLET TRUCK FEATURES

Chevrolet's special truck clutch for the 1½-ton models has a 10" disc with molded lining. Three throw-out levers assure uniform pressure on the disc and a smooth transmission of power to the rear wheels of the truck.

Chevrolet's 4-speed transmission for the 1½-ton models is greatly enlarged and strengthened. Extra pulling power is provided by the reduced gear ratio in first and reverse speeds. A larger six-bolt power take-off opening is provided.

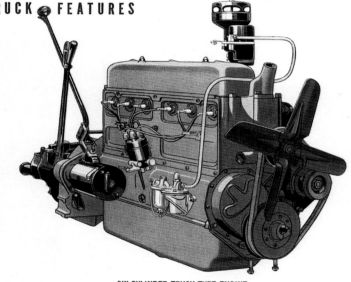

SIX-CYLINDER TRUCK-TYPE ENGINE

Down-draft carburetor, improved lubricating and cooling systems, counter-balanced crankshaft, harmonic balancer and many other advancements add to the power, speed, long life, smoothness and economy of Chevrolet's special valve-in-head six-cylinder truck engine.

Page eighteen

Above
Called the "Cast Iron Wonder," Chevrolet's overhead-valve six-cylinder debuted in 1929 to upstage Ford, which still relied on its old, archaic four-banger. Shown here is the 1932 Chevy truck six, rated at 53 horsepower.

Right
Chevrolet's own pickup legacy was slow in developing, as the company continued to let outside contractors built bodies for its half-tons well into the 1930s. Chevy first began offering steel-bodied, factory-complete roadster pickups in 1929 and continued building these soft-top trucks until 1932.

Production of Chevrolet's first trucks began in January 1918 just a few months after the fledgling Dodge Brothers firm joined Ford in the commercial vehicle market. Like their newborn rivals, Chevy's original trucks were nothing more than beefed-up cars, and they looked it. Chevrolet's car and truck lines shared front-end sheet metal until 1934, and most early models even wore the same model names as their automotive counterparts.

While initial sales were slow that first year, they soared almost tenfold in 1919. Chevrolet then needed only 10 more years to sell its first half-million trucks. By then, General Motors' low-priced division had come out of nowhere to zoom past the market's early leader, Ford.

Chevy trucks first hit the top in 1927 then fell back into second two years later. Chevrolet led again in 1933, 1934, and 1936, while Ford bounced back up in 1935 and 1937. Total Chevrolet commercial vehicle sales reached the one million milestone in 1933. That year the division also sold more trucks in the half- and one-and-a-half-ton classes than all other companies combined.

The light-duty market emerged full-force in the early 1930s, a new trend that enticed more than one truck builder to try its hand at downsizing. Before 1930, America's commercial vehicle lineup was dominated by big trucks. But the seed of change had been planted five years earlier, when Henry Ford introduced his "Model T Runabout with Pick-Up Body." Within five years, both Dodge—now a division of Chrysler Corporation—and Chevrolet followed suit with all-steel, factory-built half-tons of their own.

They were then joined in the 1930s by competing pickups from the likes of International Harvester, Studebaker, and even Mack. The Big Three, however, still stole the show 60-some years ago. More than half of the 600,000 trucks built in this country in 1937 came from Chevrolet, Ford, and Dodge. The majority of these were pickups, and most were from Chevy and Ford, leading more than one casual observer of the time to note that "Big Three" was actually a misnomer when applied to the truck business.

In truth, a more suitable name would have been the "Big Two and Dodge." From the beginning, Chevrolet and Ford ran well ahead of all rivals. Before World War II, Dodge perennially ranked a distant third and sometimes fourth as International occasionally jumped up a notch. Dodge returned to third after the war, but then fell behind International again in 1953. Sagging popularity, combined

with GMC gains, resulted in another drop to fifth, where Dodge remained for the remainder of the decade. Meanwhile, Chevrolet and Ford combined were raking in between 53 and 68 percent of annual truck sales year in, year out during the 1950s.

The Dodge Boys no longer have to worry about International, which quit the light-truck game in 1980. Nor were they ever in danger of complete collapse like Studebaker. Chrysler Corporation's perseverance in the truck market finally paid off in the 1990s, when they again found the limelight with an entirely new breed of Ram-tough pickup, a head-turning hauler that helped put the "Three" back in Big Three. Immediate responses

from Ford and Chevrolet have since made today's truck market as competitive as it has ever been.

Ford's 1925 truck largely defined the breed to the marketplace, but Ford didn't coin the term "pickup" nor originate the idea of a light-duty truck. Who did may never be established with certainty. Most manufacturers called their earliest light trucks (consisting of a cab backed by a simple open cargo box) "express delivery" or "express" models. "Pickup" apparently evolved from street slang tied to the truck's typical uses. An express delivery truck could easily pick up light loads and haul them away with haste. But "pickup" eventually replaced "express" as the generic reference for these easier-to-handle haulers—easier, that

is, than typical commercial vehicles of the day, which were designed to handle much heavier workloads.

Pickups quickly became the vehicle of choice when the business was not so big and the work not so hard. It also helped widen the existing commercial vehicle's scope by maximizing utility. Plainly put, a pickup had more uses; it wasn't as narrowly focused as a big, brawny work truck. In turn, it logically attracted more buyers. This cheaper, lighter, more socially acceptable "utility vehicle" appealed to the masses, not just captains of industry. You didn't have to be in business to own a light-duty utility vehicle, nor did you have to have arms like tree-trunks to drive one—two realities that helped usher the pickup into the transportation mainstream.

In a 1913 sales brochure, Studebaker was among the earliest manufacturers to use the term "pickup" in print. International's promotional staff used the term "pick-up," hyphenated, to describe their new S-series trucks in 1921. Popularity of the term, with hyphen, then gained real momentum in the 1930s, when the breed truly began flourishing.

Pickup popularity (more or less without the hyphen) took off big-time after the industry-wide interruption caused by World War II. Chevrolet beat all competitors to the punch with a truly new postwar pickup, not just a pre-war rehash. The resulting Advance-Design trucks, warmly welcomed in 1947, led

Above
Trucks that cost more than cars is nothing new today, but such a thing was unheard of back in 1955 when the prestigious Cameo Carrier was introduced. The Cameo on the right cost about $2,300 in 1957 before any options were added—most stickers ran much higher than that. Base price for Chevrolet's bare-bones 1957 150 sedan (left) was roughly $1,990.

Right
The camping craze of the 1960s helped spur on pickup sales to all-new heights. And in 1965, roughing it didn't come much easier than when your camper was slipped into a K-series Chevy 4x4.

the way for Ford's equally new F-1, which debuted in 1948. Ford then pushed ahead with another new design, the popular F-100, in 1953. Chevrolet retaliated in 1955 with a legend of its own, the Task-Force truck, as pretty a pickup as had ever rolled out of Detroit.

Chevy's attractively redesigned Task-Force trucks helped change the way Americans looked at pickups. Before 1955 few, if any, truck buyers cared much about appearances. Then along came the sensational Cameo Carrier to prove that style and flair could indeed peacefully coexist with utility and practicality.

The great American pickup from there slowly and surely grew even more attractive, both from an image standpoint and a practical perspective. Improved engineering in the 1960s made light trucks even easier to drive, and Chevrolet trucks were right there on the cutting edge. Pickups evolved in the public perception from work vehicles that could stand in for other driving, to all-around transportation of the most practical sort. While Ford did finally take over the sales lead in the 1970s, Chevy's truck builders have by no means remained content playing second fiddle. On the contrary, 80 years and counting and the race is far from over.

Above
In base form, Chevrolet's new pickup for 1967 was attractive and more comfortable than previous models. Adding the new Custom Sport Truck option further enhanced the attraction with extra trim and a bucket-seat interior. This CST is one of 12,588 built for 1967.

Left
Among Chevrolet's latest, greatest trucks is the new Avalanche, an unprecedented combination of pickup and sport-ute. This quick-change artist was introduced in 2001 as a 2002 model.

GMC *Kissin' Cousins*

GMC and Chevrolet truck lines began merging in the 1930s, although the former always retained their position as a notch or two up on the prestige scale. After World War II, Pontiac engines and upscale trim became GMC standards. And GMC also produced a Suburban model. Shown here are 1963 GMC offerings.

Chevrolet and Ford battled back and forth for the truck industry's sales lead all through the 1930s, but the Bow-Tie gang put a headlock on the top spot just before World War II. When wartime restrictions affected civilian vehicle production in early 1942, Chevrolet was ahead of Ford, followed by International and Dodge. Right behind Dodge was Chevy's corporate cousin, GMC.

Commonly lost in the shadows of those hundreds of thousands of Chevrolet trucks sold each year, GMC rose as high as fourth when Dodge dropped off badly during the second-half of the 1950s. Fifth-place had been GMC's traditional spot before the war, but the company became friends with fourth well into the 1960s before Chrysler's truck division finally recovered and took back third-place in the 1970s. International began to fade early in the 1970s, and allowed GMC to move back up to fourth again.

Long before all that leapfrogging took place, GMC trucks had contributed their fair share of milestones to the commercial vehicle market. Historic breakthroughs include many "firsts" such as four-wheel brakes, two-speed rear axle, recirculating ball-bearing steering, dual-range transmission, full-pressure lubrication and hydraulic lifters for its engines, and air suspension. GMC was also the first to offer a left-leg-friendly Synchromesh transmission for heavy truck applications.

Over its long, rich history, GMC has built everything from pickups and big rigs, to taxis and buses. GMC's history is nowhere near as cut and dried as Chevrolet's. The complex GMC legacy began in 1909 when GM founder William Durant bought up two Michigan-based truck builders, the Rapid Motor Vehicle Company and the Reliance Motor Car Company, as part of his early plans to build a manufacturing empire like none ever seen before. Founded in Detroit by local inventor Max Grabowsky in 1902, Rapid was among the first American transportation manufacturers to concentrate solely on commercial vehicles. Many early trucks debuted as sideline products to their parent company's automobile line. Others were still simply based on beefed-up automotive chassis. Not so for Rapid's offerings. These were trucks through and through, a fact not lost on prospective customers. Quick success in the marketplace led to the construction of a new, larger Rapid plant in Pontiac, Michigan, in 1905.

The Reliance firm, founded in Owosso, Michigan, introduced a two-cylinder passenger car in 1904. Two years later the company dropped out of the automobile business after the introduction of its first commercial vehicle. Similar to Rapid, Reliance built only trucks from then on, and both companies built the same trucks, complete with Rapid and Reliance badges, even after they became part of Durant's GM universe.

Initially the General Motors Truck Company was formed to oversee sales of Rapid and Reliance trucks. An officially trademarked GMC label first appeared in 1911, and the Rapid and Reliance nameplates were dropped the following year. The first commercial vehicle to wear a GMC badge appeared at the New York auto show in 1912. GMC truck production was then centralized at the big Pontiac plant in 1913. Medium- and heavy-duty models represented the main priorities early on.

General Motors' Pontiac Division introduced a half-ton panel delivery truck in 1927. This identical platform was then marketed as GMC's light-truck T-11 model in 1928. A T-series half-ton "express" model was also introduced. While the new T-11 pickups wore GMC badges and shared sheetmetal with Chevrolet's light-trucks, they remained in touch with their heritage beneath the skin. Power came from Pontiac's 185.6-ci six-cylinder.

GMC pickups began to look more and more like their Chevrolet running mates as the 1930s progressed, but Pontiac-based engines remained the prominent power choice up through the 1960s. When GM's radically restyled 1955 pickups were fitted with ground-breaking overhead-valve V-8s, Chevy's trucks were fitted with the milestone 265-ci small-block, and GMC half-tons received Pontiac's lesser-known 287-ci V-8. The idea was to set GMC's light-trucks apart from Chevrolet's trucks. As the story goes, the Pontiac engine supposedly supplied the GMC pickup with a tad more prestige. This distinction, however, all but disappeared by 1970 when GMC's light-trucks truly became badge-engineered Chevys.

Forty years earlier the thought of a "prestigious pickup" had yet to be imagined. At the same time, GMC pickups were few and far between as the division concentrated on the construction of heavy trucks, buses, and such. The light-duty T-11 was dropped after 1932, and no half-tons were offered in 1933 and 1934. GMC returned to the light-truck market in 1935 with a three-quarter-ton truck. A half-ton truck reappeared the following year with the modern streamlined styling introduced by Chevrolet pickups in 1934. By 1937, both lines were sharing comparable sheetmetal. From then on it was extra trim, bolder grilles, a few extra interior baubles, and some top-shelf engineering features that set the GMC apart from its Chevrolet counterparts.

Chevrolet and GMC also shared various specialty models, including the Suburban and Cameo Carrier. The latter was known as the "Suburban pickup" on GMC's side of the fence, and this classy truck was built in very small numbers into 1959. Chevy's Cameo retired in 1958.

If there was one moment when GMC truly did outshine its corporate cousin, it was in 1991 when the former unveiled the Syclone pickup, which was easily the hottest thing to ever drop a tailgate to that point. With 280 turbocharged horses, this all-wheel-drive sport truck could scream from 0 to 60 miles per hour in only 4.9 seconds. The Typhoon appeared in 1992 with the Syclone's high-performance V-6 to help put the "sport" in sport-utility.

Today, GMC's pickup and sport-utes rank among the truck industry's best-looking and smartest buys.

GMC was chosen to be the official truck for the 1974 Indianapolis 500. Along with the various pickups and vans sent to the Brickyard in May 1974 for support-vehicle duty, about 1,000 half-ton replicas were sold through GMC dealers.

GMC truck roots date back to 1902, the year the Rapid Motor Vehicle Company opened its doors. Both the Rapid firm and the Reliance Motor Car Company were

bought up by GM founder William Durant in 1909, and the two eventually evolved into the General Motors Truck Company. The Rapid and Reliance nameplates were dropped in 1912.

GMC people were proud as hell of their automatic-equipped trucks, introduced in 1953. The optional Hyrdra-Matic automatic transmission didn't become a Chevy pickup option until 1954.

15

Bow-Tie Beginnings

Chevrolet Trucks Debut in 1918

Above
A Chevrolet sales manager poses proudly with the first Model 490 passenger car, introduced in 1916. The car's name came from its affordable price tag—$490

Left
The one-ton Model T introduced in 1918, was based on the FA-series passenger car. This is a 1920 Model T with canopy express bodywork.

By 1918 the fledgling car company founded by William Crapo Durant in November 1911 was as solid as a rock, even though the popular French race driver who lent his name (as well as his proven mechanical expertise) to the young firm was long gone. Louis Chevrolet had envisioned his moniker emblazoned on the nose of higher-priced, high-performance automobiles. Billy Durant was eyeing the broader market, which Henry Ford's low-priced, highly successful Model T had come to dominate since its introduction in October 1908. Durant and Chevrolet clashed continually until the race driver quit in disgust in September 1913. Durant kept the Chevrolet name, however, which he had secured for the company by contract. The proud Frenchman drifted into relative obscurity, but his name under Durant's care would grow to worldwide recognition.

The market proved that Durant was right: Chevrolet Motor Company was better off competing in the low-priced, mass-production field than in the smaller, upscale segment. In truth, Durant wanted to be on top; he just had a broader view of how to get there. Durant had founded General Motors in 1908, only to be removed in 1910 by bankers alarmed at his wild expansion. His dream with Chevrolet was to make another fortune and buy his way back into GM. Producing and selling low-cost cars on a grand scale was how he planned to do it.

The plan worked perfectly. Almost overnight Chevrolet carved out its own niche. Company coffers were already filling up nicely when the Model 490 appeared, in prototype form, in January 1915. Officially labeled a 1916 model, the Model 490 took its name from its attractive price tag, $490, same as old Henry's Model T. Affordability guaranteed success; within 17 days after officially going on sale on June 1, 1915, the Model 490 inspired 46,611 orders worth $23 million. By the end of the year, Chevrolet's working capital totaled $7.5 million, its stock was valued at $20 million, and there was more coming.

Model year production for 1916 jumped nearly fivefold to more than 70,000. Annual sales the next year surpassed the 125,000 mark. Meanwhile, Durant was putting all his newfound money where his heart was—back into General Motors. After gaining control of 54.5 percent of GM's stock, he marched right in and grabbed the big corporation's reigns in September 1915. Three years later, on May 2, 1918, he brought Chevrolet into the General Motors fold.

Introduced in 1918, the Model 490 half-ton truck was based on the low-cost Chevrolet automobile of the same name and sold sans bodywork. Custom wooden cabs, like the one on this 1918 half-ton, were either built by the buyer or purchased from an aftermarket supplier.

Left
While most cabs seen in the 1910s were of the open C-type, the bulk of the wooden bodywork bolted onto Chevy truck frames back then was nowhere near this ornate.

Below
One distinct advantage the early Chevy trucks had over their Ford rivals involved the use of a more modern sliding-gear transmission with its conventional pedal arrangement—clutch on left, brake on right. Ford's archaic planetary transmission relied on clunky foot-pedal controls.

The rest is history, as was Billy Durant just a few short years down the road. His enthusiastic expansion plans once more got him into trouble, this time with a lot of help from an economic recession. After GM stock nose-dived in 1920, angry stockholders forced a corporate reorganization in which Durant was shown the door a second time. Although he did recover and build yet another, albeit much smaller, automotive empire, the man who laid the foundation for Detroit's greatest conglomerate never made it back to the top. He was finally done in by the Depression in 1932. Then, like Louis Chevrolet, Durant found obscurity. Louis died in 1941; Billy six years later.

Chevrolet nearly expired as well not long after Durant's second ousting. The corporation's new leadership considered killing the low-priced car, but Alfred Sloan, Jr., would have none of that. Sloan, the big man brought in to sort through the mess left behind by Durant, argued against ending the young Bow-Tie bloodline. Instead, Sloan believed, it was the remaining "Durant officers" who deserved the axe. Sloan cleaned house and redirected Chevrolet toward a more promising future—where Chevrolet could run with Ford without directly taking it on. Chevy found a niche with a slightly higher per-vehicle cost than its rival from Dearborn. But those extra dollars bought a little more refinement, a little more comfort, a little more car.

Chevrolet's quest to unseat its rival gained new momentum in 1924, when Ford's former production

manager, William S. Knudsen, came aboard as the division's new president and general manager. Ford sold eight vehicles for every one Chevrolet sold in 1924, but just one year later that ratio dropped to 4:1. In 1926 it was less than 3:1. These figures included cars and trucks.

Sloan may have dumped Durant's men like yesterday's trash in 1920, but he chose to recycle one of Billy's visions: Chevrolet's future simply had to include trucks along with cars if the division was going to compete with the Blue Oval boys. Henry Ford had cast that reality in stone when he decided to offer a factory-built truck in 1917. Dodge had helped to up the ante by introducing its first truck later that year. Chevy officials were left with one choice: jump on the bandwagon or eat dust.

That jump appeared far more frightening in 1918 than it did a decade or so later. Trucks, at least "light" trucks, were a new market species when the Big Three players began feeling their way into the commercial-vehicle field. As late as 1922 *Automotive Industries* was reporting "that the truck has not yet found its exact

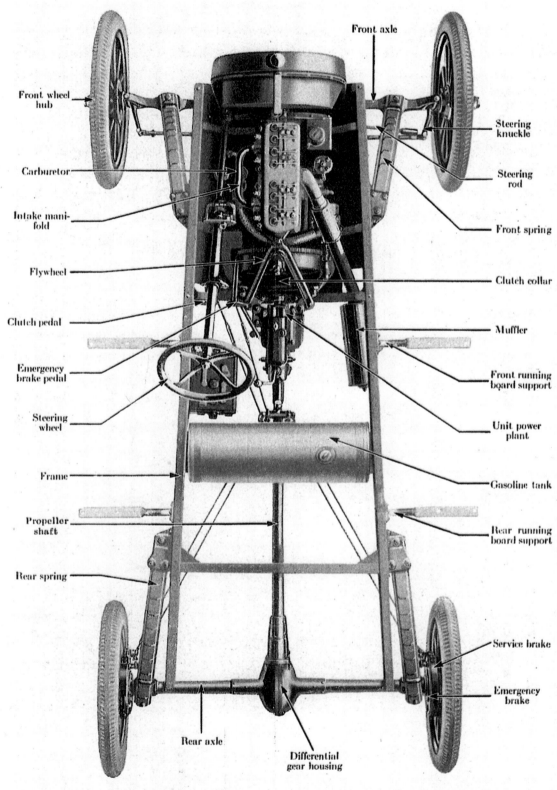

Front axle

Front wheel hub

Carburetor

Intake manifold

Flywheel

Clutch pedal

Emergency brake pedal

Steering wheel

Frame

Propeller shaft

Rear spring

Rear axle

Differential gear housing

Steering knuckle

Steering rod

Front spring

Clutch collar

Muffler

Front running board support

Unit power plant

Gasoline tank

Rear running board support

Service brake

Emergency brake

Plan view of Chevrolet chassis—showing and locating all important units as assembled, and displaying effectively the advanced type of Chevrolet cantilever springs

Left
Both Model 490s used the same chassis and powertrain, with the one major difference being the heavier rear springs fitted to the half-ton truck. This is a plan view of the 1917 Model 490 automobile platform.

Far left
Both Model 490s, car and truck, shared the same overhead-valve four-cylinder in 1918. Displacement was 171 cubic inches, horsepower was 26.

Middle left
With few differences between the two, Chevrolet's first half-ton simply shared its model designation, 490, with the car it was based on.

niche in transportation and that further development will be necessary before it attains its maximum possibilities." Of course, Ford, Chevrolet and Dodge weren't known as the "Big Three" then, but the trio didn't eventually become so tremendous by failing to respond whenever opportunity knocked—and it certainly was knocking in 1918.

Although trucks were not exactly "niched," they were not a whimsical experiment, either. The Great War, then nearing its end, had proven that these heavy-duty, internal-combustion haulers could perform alongside the old, dependable packhorse. Even before World War I, annual truck production had nearly kept stride

Above
Chevrolet's Model T one-ton truck was based on this automobile, the FA. FA-series Chevy cars also debuted in 1918.

Right
The FA-series passenger car frame was stretched 17 inches (to a total of 125) for duty beneath the Model T one-ton truck. Chevy's first Model T wore a $1,325 price tag in bare-chassis form in 1918.

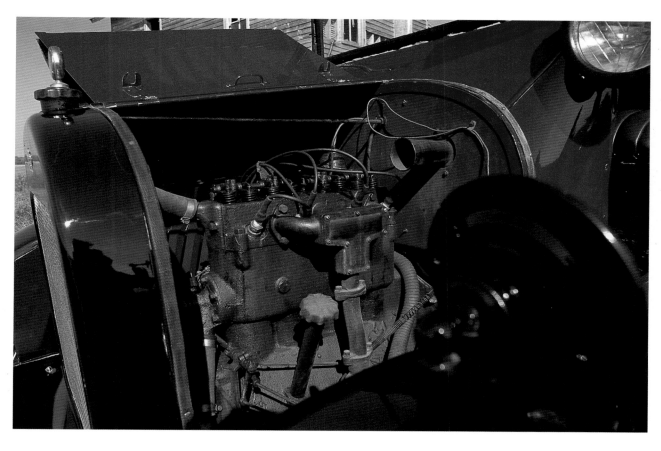

Above
What a joy it must have been to live in the days before lawyers ruled the world. Nary an eye blinked when Chevrolet "borrowed" Henry Ford's famous moniker for its one-ton truck in 1918.

Left
The Model T truck used the bigger FA-series four-cylinder, a 224-ci OHV powerplant rated at 37 horsepower.

with its automotive counterpart, growing 483 percent from 1912 to 1917, compared to 489 percent for cars. Each vehicle type was searching for its most promising role in the evolving motorized world. It was clear that the automobile was bound for greatness, but the truck's future was not so certain.

Truck production in 1917 reached a new peak of 128,157 units. The same year, 1,740,792 cars were produced. During any given year before 1923, cars outsold trucks by at least a 10:1 ratio. In some years the odds that a new vehicle chugging around a bend was a truck ran as low as 20:1. Early industry analysts could easily predict that the demand for commercial vehicles naturally would continue ramping upward. But most figured that trucks would never account for more than a 10-percent wedge of the motor-vehicle pie. Half of that pie—as the truck market makes up today—was a possibility no one could have envisioned, even in their wildest dreams, 80 years ago.

In the horseless carriage's early days, many automotive entrepreneurs probably considered building trucks.

As pioneering automobile writer David Wells observed in 1907, "while many firms are manufacturing delivery wagons and trucks to the capacity of their plants, the possibilities for commercial vehicles have hardly begun to be exploited."

Yet, various factors worked in concert to limit the truck market before the 1920s came along to help change all the rules. First off, light-duty vehicles were not conceived early on. The great majority of commercial vehicles built before 1914 or so were hulking, super-heavy-duty, expectedly high-priced, hairy beasts—not the type of machines that just anyone would be in the market to buy. America's first big truck builders—Autocar, White, Mack, Diamond T, and Federal, to name a prominent few—only built really big trucks. Two of the most successful firms prior to 1920, REO and International Harvester, did dabble in some lighter trucks, as well as a lot of cars (REO) and tons of tractors (International). Even as late as 1925, a one-ton truck was considered "light." Three-quarter-tonners were rare before then, and the half-ton pickup was all but unheard of.

Big Three | *Birth of the Truck Market*

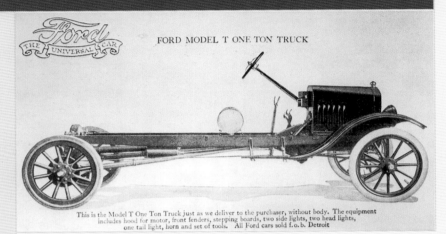

FORD MODEL T ONE TON TRUCK

This is the Model T One Ton Truck just as we deliver to the purchaser, without body. The equipment includes hood for motor, front fenders, stepping boards, two side lights, two head lights, one tail light, horn and set of tools. All Ford cars sold f.o.b. Detroit

Ford's truck legacy began in 1917 with the introduction of the Model T truck, better known as the Model TT, with the second T signifying its one-ton load rating. The Model TT was sold just as you see here, with its chassis in want of a body.

The pickup truck is a legendary American icon. Even today with many imported nameplates such as Nissan and Toyota, the essence behind the pickup truck remains true red, white, and blue. Especially considering that all of those "imports" are now built right here in America.

The Far East's earliest attempts to jump on this Western bandwagon initially gained momentum when it capitalized on an untapped market that U.S. manufacturers had only toyed with before. In 1958 Nissan's alter-ego, Datsun, introduced America to its first viable compact pickup, a breed that later found real favor in the 1970s during the gasoline crisis. Even though they were easier on the wallet at the pump and off a dealer's lot, compact imports still didn't pose any real threat to domestic incumbents. Plainly put, America's Big Three continued to build full-size pickups. Challenges from both abroad and here at home have come and gone, but Chevrolet, Ford, and Dodge have still managed to keep on truckin'.

The Big Three truck race dates back to 1917, about a year before Chevrolet entered the fray. The light-truck market we all take for granted today was officially originated by Ford in 1917. While Ford trucks were seen on the road before then, nearly all of those primitive forerunners were aftermarket conversions. Many "mom and pop" companies had sprung up before World War I to supply Model T owners with conversion kits to transform their

Ford is credited with creating the American pickup truck in 1925. This Model T Runabout was the first factory-built, steel-bodied half-ton truck.

Flivvers into light-duty utility vehicles or heavy-duty one-ton haulers. Henry Ford grew tired outside firms profiting from his products. On June 27, 1917, Dearborn officials announced the production of Ford's first factory-built truck, the Model TT one-ton chassis.

Dodge Brothers had also manufactured some trucks before Ford introduced its Model TT, but these appeared in 1916-1917 for military duty only. Dodge rolled out its first civilian "truck" in October 1917 as a 1918 model. This half-ton machine was initially called a "commercial car." The vehicle was basically a full-roofed delivery van with wire screens in place of panels in back. The appropriately named "Screenside" was not much more than a Dodge automobile behind the screens. Its cargo-carrying body, heavier springs, and larger tires set it apart from its more civilized counterpart.

A common practice during the pickup's earliest days was to beef up a passenger-car chassis and retain some automotive body parts. As for the aftermarket body business, it remained a viable interest well into the 1930s. This cottage industry didn't begin to curdle until after Ford rolled out another trucking milestone. Ford's "Model T Runabout with Pick-Up Body" was introduced in April 1925 and wasn't much more than a Model T roadster with a small cargo box mounted in place of the car's rear deck. Nonetheless, this combination is widely recognized as America's first true pickup. Light-duty pickups had existed before 1925, but not one was factory built that featured nearly all wooden bodywork. Ford's 1925 Model T half-ton truck broke ground because it was sold complete from the factory with all-steel bodywork. No more middlemen nor carpenters were needed.

Although another "factory-built" pickup from Dodge had actually appeared the year before, it failed to qualify for milestone status due to various technicalities. This heavier three-quarter-ton truck featured a wooden body supplied by Graham Brothers, Dodge's Indiana-based truck division. Dodge's first all-steel half-ton pickup arrived in 1929 immediately after Walter Chrysler added the well-respected firm to his own burgeoning empire.

By then the Big Three was locked in and loaded, and the half-ton pickup that we all know and love today was also off and running. Pickup popularity truly exploded after World War II. Total truck sales hovered around the 1 million mark in 1960, and surpassed 2 million in 1971. The market share hit 20 percent the following year. Thirty years later, cars and trucks share almost equal billing—and to think it all began with a bare-chassis bruiser back in 1917.

Dodge Brothers teamed up with their Graham Brothers affiliate in 1924 to offer this full-bodied three-quarter-ton pickup. Its cargo box was made of wood.

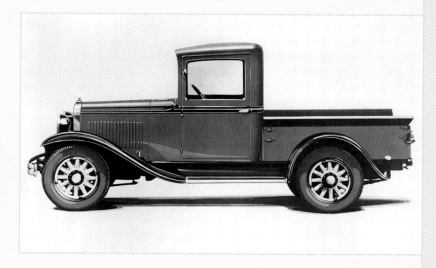

Walter Chrysler bought the Brothers firm in 1928 and immediately brought full production of Dodge pickups "in-house." This 1929 Dodge was the company's first factory-built, steel-bodied half-ton.

Though it was introduced very late in 1917, Dodge Brothers' first "truck"—actually called a commercial car—was still considered a 1917 model by parent company officials. The 1917 Dodge was called a "screenside" thanks to those wire screens in back.

Above
Chevrolet's heavy-duty Model T was fitted with a worm-drive rear axle, a strong but slow and clunky setup that contributed to the truck's feeble top end. A Monarch governor limited speed to 25 miles per hour.

Right top
Chevrolet briefly tried to expand its truck line, introducing the three-quarter-ton Model G in 1921. Featuring the Model 490's engine in a shortened Model T frame (complete with worm-drive), the Model G was built for two years only. This is the 1922 version.

Right bottom
Various aftermarket firms offered this clever conversion for Chevrolet roadsters in the 1920s. The cargo box simply slipped right into the trunk after the deck lid was removed. These roadster pickup conversions were still around in the 1930s. This example is from 1926.

Chassis · · $745
With Cab $820
With Exp. Body · · $855

CHEVROLET

"G" LIGHT TRUCK
A sturdy new model especially designed for reliable and economical service for all light hauling requirements

$920
Express Body and Top f.o.b. Flint, Mich.

Even harder to find 75 years ago was a rocket scientist. Yet if you did scare one up then—and his name probably would have' been Goddard—he might 'have explained, in painstaking detail, that you didn't need him to tell you that diversity represented the obvious key to more rapid expansion of the commercial vehicle market. Light trucks were needed to balance out their bigger brethren, widen the commercial vehicle's scope, and make hauling the goods easier and more affordable to folks who maybe didn't have all that many goods to haul—or a whole lot of time to haul them away.

All early trucks, regardless of size, were brain-numbingly slow. That was no big deal for the big rigs built specifically to handle large, heavy loads. Speed then was traded off for brute strength. But what about the farmer hoping to rush his fresh load of produce to the market 50 miles away? Or the launderer trying to deliver his lightweight stock of garments across town on time? These potential truck buyers needed quicker, lighter, cheaper-to-operate vehicles. Horses, railroads, big Macks—they simply wouldn't do.

But even if the speedier, lower-priced, lightweight pickup had appeared prior to World War I, America wasn't ready to exploit its merits. Two major problems prevented the pickup from emerging earlier than it did, and both could be found where the rubber met the ground: crude tires and even cruder roads.

Like early horseless carriages, nearly all trucks rolled on solid rubber prior to World War I. The pneumatic tire—one of the first great technological advancements in personal-transportation history—was patented by John Dunlop in 1888 and appeared on most motorcars by 1900. While "riding on air" made cars more comfortable and helped increase top speeds, all early tube tires were easily punctured and wore out quickly. Fixing flats was a regular—and time consuming—routine for the pioneering motorist. Much more durable and comparatively maintenance-free, slow-poke solid tires remained the best choice for truck owners well into the 1910s—but the rough, slow ride limited what truckers could haul, and how quickly.

Knox trucks, introduced in 1902, were among the earliest to use pneumatic tires, which were enhanced around 1907 with non-skid tread designs. In 1913 Goodrich advanced the technology with a tougher

They could brag all they wanted about the ever-increasing dimensions inside a Chevrolet truck cab in 1928. But the plain fact remained that these vehicles were cramped, to say the least.

cotton-cord inner structure that essentially tripled tire life. It was then left to Firestone in 1922 to roll out the first low-pressure "balloon" tire, a revolutionary breakthrough that both ushered in modern tire technology and made Ford's Model T an even better buy in 1923. With a wider, lower profile and less than half the air pressure of its predecessors, the new balloon tires improved ride comfort exponentially and made higher speeds possible, as Firestone would prove over and over again at the Indianapolis 500 during the late 1920s.

That, however, was at The Brickyard, where there were no ruts, bogs, or washouts—just a wide, hard track surface. The real world was not so accommodating. While brick streets were present in most cities early in the twentieth century, the vast majority of American highways and back roads before World War I were rough, dusty routes that quickly turned into car-swallowing quagmires at the slightest touch of precipitation.

This country's first concrete pavement was laid down in Bellefontaine, Ohio, in 1893. Yet, by 1914 there were still fewer than 13,000 miles of paved highways across the United States. Seven years later, officials counted 3.2 million miles of American highways, but only 14 percent of that total was surfaced. Even as late as 1926, Mississippi could only claim 200 miles of paved

road for the entire state. Wyoming that year only had 50 miles, Montana 35.

A report in *Automotive Industries* from January 1918 noted that "Since the truck has proved its position as an essential to the successful conduct of war overseas and has been tried out under extreme conditions in time of national commercial stress at home, there can be no question as to its assured future." But that future, the report continued, demanded "a highway system which will furnish the opportunity for unlimited truck-mileage irrespective of weather conditions. . . . Given reasonably good highways, the railroad short- and middle-distance hauls are things of the past. Good roads will enable the truck user to reach points which are now commercially inaccessible—good roads mean more, and yet more, trucks."

A public outcry for better roads reached a crescendo in 1918. In response, more than 20 highway bills were introduced the following year in the 66th Congress proposing, among other things, a federal highway commission and a national highway network. By 1919 all states had formed their own individual highway departments. Two years later the Federal Highway Act of 1921 established the foundation for a modernized nationwide road system. From then on, Washington would cover half the construction costs on designated "Federal Aid" road projects. Of the 26,000 miles of national road construction planned for 1928, 21,000 of those miles qualified for federal funding. In 1928, President Dwight Eisenhower's Interstate Highway Act was still 28 years in the future, but the 1921 act was a start.

Most witnesses by 1920 recognized that a modernized national highway network would create a "trickle-down" effect. That is, secondary roads too would expand and improve as better main arteries increased the need (and want) for a stronger feeder system. It was the establishment of more accessible rural routes that truly opened the gate for the emergence of the light-duty pickup. Better roads meant there was a need more trucks that could now run faster. Thus, the commercial vehicle's attraction grew and its scope widened.

A few truck companies were promoting cutting-edge swiftness as early as 1915—REO's legendary Speedwagon comes quickly to mind. These vehicles were mostly one-ton machines (there were some three-quarter-tonners) that still carried relatively heavy price tags and required real men to drive them. "Speed" too remained a relative term. Thirty miles per hour was about as fast as it got during the big "speed truck's" heyday in the 1920s. Though attractive in their day, the speed truck set remained limited, and the bigger, even slower one-and-a-half-ton truck continued plodding along as the predominant choice among commercial vehicle customers.

When Henry Ford kicked off the Big Three truck rivalry in 1917, he did so with a burly one-ton, the Model TT. Dodge's first truck was a half-ton "commercial car." Although Chevrolet was the last to enter the game, it was afforded the opportunity to call both hands. Chevy truck production began in St. Louis in January 1918 with a well-played pair: a one-ton and a half-ton. Like their Ford and Dodge counterparts, these new trucks were based on modified automotive platforms.

Derived from Chevrolet's new-for-1918 FA-series passenger car, the big one-ton Model T truck rested on a stretched FA frame (wheelbase was 125 inches, compared to the car line's 108), wore a $1,325 price tag, and never once apologized to Henry Ford for "lifting" its name. That price did not include a cab or body, as was the case with Henry's Model TT one-ton chassis, which sold for a mere $600. Chevrolet delivered its Model T truck with only a hood, cowl, fenders and short running boards. Adding the rest was the customer's prerogative.

While two complete models—the $1,460 flareboard express and a covered express priced at $1,545—were listed for the Model T one-ton in 1918, these cabs and bodies were supplied by aftermarket suppliers and typically installed by dealers, not the factory. Customers who purchased the bare-bones Model T either constructed their own cab and bed or they looked to that same aftermarket. Before 1930 there were many different cab/body types (essentially all made of wood) offered separately by various independent manufacturers, including Hercules, Superior, Columbia, and Mifflinburg.

Far and away the number one supplier of cab/body types was the Martin-Parry Company of Indianapolis, Chevrolet's own "favorite" contractor. Martin-Parry supplied the great majority of those dealer-installed cabs and bodies advertised early-on in Chevy truck brochures. While that advertising material didn't promote the Indiana firm exclusively—Hercules was also commonly

"Factory-equipped" closed cabs began appearing on Chevrolet trucks in 1925. This one-ton flatbed Chevy is a 1927 model.

THE CHEVROLET LIGHT DELIVERY

2 The Light Delivery Truck you buy must have sturdiness and strength

For thousand-pound loads, the Chevrolet Light Delivery Truck supplies a delivery service of utmost reliability and economy.

It is compact in design, sturdy in construction, and offers fast, light, dependable delivery service at a remarkably low initial cost.

FOR ECONOMICAL TRANSPORTATION

Most Chevrolet trucks were still sold without bodywork up through the 1920s. This is what a half-ton Chevy truck looked like when it left the factory in 1928.

mentioned—the ever-present fine print always seemed to include "body as built by Martin-Parry and others." Hercules bodies remained popular into the 1930s even after Chevrolet began offering factory-complete pickups right off the assembly line. Martin-Parry built so much bodywork so well during the 1920s, GM bought out the company in 1930, after which time Chevrolet effectively began fashioning its own bodies in a big way.

Like its Model T running mate, Chevrolet's new half-ton for 1918 also was marketed sans bodywork. Unlike its one-ton big brother, the smaller truck's chassis was only mildly modified, so little, in fact, that the machine retained the name of the car it was based on: Model 490. Priced at $595, Chevrolet's 1918 light truck used a basically unchanged Model 490 automobile frame with its 102-inch wheelbase. The only real modification came in back, where heavier quarter-elliptical leaf springs beefed things up to that 1,000-pound capacity rating.

The Model 490 truck used a conventional drop-forged I-beam front axle also suspended by quarter-elliptical leaf springs. The rear axle was of the three-quarter-floating variety; it featured Hyatt roller bearings carried on the wheel hub and in the axle housing, not on the shaft itself. Wheels and tires were 12-spoke wooden "artillery" type shod with 30 x 3.5-inch pneumatic treads—again the same as the 490 passenger car. Brakes were 10-inch drums at the rear wheels only.

Both 490 vehicles also shared powertrains, beginning with a 26-horsepower, 171-ci overhead-valve four-cylinder fed by a Zenith one-barrel carburetor and sparked by a Remy ignition system. Behind that four was a cone clutch and Chevrolet's superior selective-shift, sliding-gear three-speed transmission, a major advantage compared to Ford's archaic foot-pedal-controlled planetary gearbox.

It was that more cooperative transmission—combined with the pneumatic tires on both its half- and one-ton trucks—that supplied promotional people with the fodder they needed to put Chevrolet's first commercial vehicles on the map. By 1923, ads bragged of "the lowest-priced quality trucks in the world capable of fast heavy-duty service." The fact that Chevy's Model T actually cost more than twice as much as Ford's Model TT apparently didn't count; the operative term was "capable of fast heavy-duty service." While the Model T truck was no speed demon, its standard pneumatic tires allowed it to haul greater loads at higher speeds with less wear and tear on both the chassis and driver. Ford kept its costs down by, among other things, installing solid rear tires on its early Model TT. Much more expensive pneumatics didn't appear until 1919, and even then they were still optional.

Cost also took prominence over quality by way of Ford's continued use of its obsolete, comparatively clunky planetary transmission. According to ads, the selective three-speed in Chevrolet trucks allowed drivers to "run the motor at the most economical speed under all conditions." This advantage inspired the company's prime advertising motto for the 1920s. By 1926 Chevrolet was "the world's largest builder of gear-shift trucks." A "modern" sliding-gear transmission didn't replace that old, tired planetary unit in Ford light trucks until the Model A superseded the equally old and tired Model T in 1928.

Chevrolet's first Model T truck and Ford's Model TT did share one "old-world" engineering feature—both used simple yet strong, durable yet speed-limiting "worm-drive" rear axles. As late as 1919, 66 percent of new trucks still featured worm-drive rear ends.

Chevrolet beat Ford in improving this feature. First, the 1922 Model 490 line was treated to an improved beveled ring-and-pinion in place of the old, gnarly, straight-cut gears previously used. Still a noisy annoyance, this setup then was replaced in 1925 by a one-piece, "banjo-style" differential unit with spiral-bevel gears. Again, it wasn't until the Model A arrived in 1928 that more modern differentials began finding their way beneath Ford light-delivery models. Nineteen-twenty-eight was also the last year for worm-drive in Ford's heavier trucks. Chevrolet had dropped the worm-drive axle cold-turkey after 1922.

The rarely seen Model G, a three-quarter-ton truck that Chevrolet had introduced only the prior year had also been dropped in 1922. According to company brochures, the Model G was "the product of years of experience." It combined the Model 490's engine and front sheet metal with the Model T's heavier frame (on a 120-inch wheelbase instead of 125) and worm-drive rear axle. Chevy hoped to serve customers who wanted a smaller-capacity truck with the strength and performance of larger models. Demand for the Model G never materialized, however. Production in 1921 was 855, followed by a mere 273 the following year.

The first Model T one-ton used a bigger four-cylinder engine borrowed, like its chassis, from Chevrolet's FA-series automobile. It was the same 224-ci four-cylinder, with a governor added to limit the Model T's top speed to 25 miles per hour. Output was 37 horsepower.

Total 1918 production for both models was about 900. Once word got around, there was no stopping the Chevrolet truck, especially the Model 490. As sales catalogs explained in 1920, "the Chevrolet Light Delivery Wagon was designed to meet the requirements of those who have need of a commercial car with slightly less capacity and of considerably lighter weight than is afforded by a one-ton truck." With the 490 leading the way, Chevy truck production soared to more than 8,000 in 1919.

Yet, truck buyers really didn't know how much they wanted much lighter, faster half-ton pickups until Henry

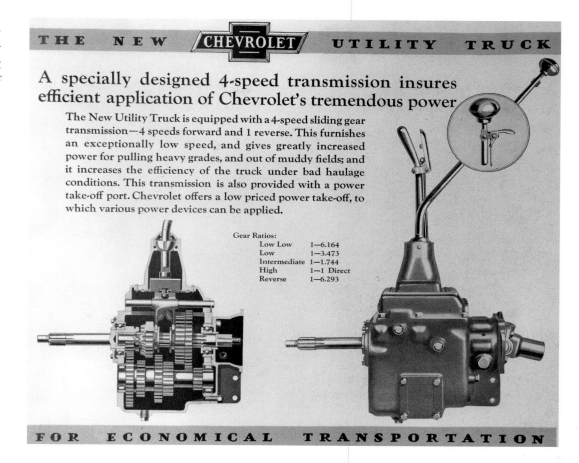

Ford rolled out America's first all-steel, factory-complete example in 1925. Detroit then discovered just how easy it could be to sell trucks in really big numbers, and the light-truck market began to gel. A February 1925 article in *Automotive Industries* observed: "While trucks still are a small proportion of the total motor vehicle output, their relative strength in the 1924 market is significant of the facility with which these vehicles are fitting into their rightful place in our transportation scheme."

In 1924, 81.4 percent of new trucks sold were one-and-one-half-ton models or smaller, with that "smaller" group making up only a tiny sliver of this segment. The figure the following year was 86.3 percent, as the really big boys (two-tons and up) began losing ground. Their little brothers, meanwhile, were just starting to roll. For 1926, the market slice for trucks of three-quarter-ton capacity or less measured 13 percent. That bottom-end piece of the pie grew to 21.9 percent four years later, signaling the solidification of the pickup field. The Big Three's light trucks not only flourished in the 1930s,

A heavy-duty four-speed transmission appeared for Chevrolet's heavier trucks in 1928.

Though still of "mechanical" design, the four-wheel brakes introduced for Chevy trucks in 1928 represented real progress.

Chevrolet's large, positive 4-wheel brakes, with 317 sq. in. of braking surface will stop the heaviest laden truck with ease

Chevrolet offers a separate rear wheel emergency brake

The New Utility Truck is equipped with large 4-wheel brakes, with an entirely separate, independently operated set of emergency brakes on the rear wheels. The total braking area is 317 square inches, insuring quick, positive stops in any service or emergency.

The front wheel brakes are of the internal expanding type and are provided with simple adjustments.

The rear wheel service brake is the external contracting type, and the emergency brake the internal expanding type.

FOR ECONOMICAL TRANSPORTATION

they also inspired various new rivals, from Mack to Crosley, to join them.

Ford truck sales still ranked well ahead of Chevy's in the early 1920s. On June 3, 1925, Chevrolet's 100,000th truck rolled off the line. Ford had built that many Model TT one-tons alone by 1919 and picked up the pace further after the half-ton Model T roadster appeared six years later. Dearborn sold more than 33,000 soft-top pickups in 1925. That number on its own topped Chevrolet's entire truck line total that year.

Then came 1927. Though the challenger did receive a little help—Henry Ford basically shut his company down while preparing the Model A for its 1928 introduction—a win was a win; amazing as it seemed, Chevrolet was indeed the world's largest builder of trucks, period. Chevy trucks remained number one in 1928 before Ford rose back up to reclaim its place atop the heap.

Chevrolet had risen to the top in two quick leaps that had come hot on the heels of William Knudsen's

arrival in January 1924. The new division president had one main goal: to match Ford in sales one-for-one. Chevy trucks were soon doing their part: 1926 sales soared by more than 300 percent to a record of roughly 77,350 units. Another record followed in 1927 as that year's final tally jumped another 67 percent and the 100,000 annual sales plateau was surpassed for the first time. In 1929 Chevrolet built its 500,000th commercial vehicle since its humble beginnings 11 years before.

Various updates and advancements typically dotted that span. Most noticeable were the many moniker modifications. Chevrolet last used the 490 and T designations in 1922. In 1923 the entire truck line took on the "Superior" title, the same name used by Chevrolet automobiles that year. A trend then developed as Chevy trucks and cars continued sharing names in 1927 (Capitol), 1928 (National), and 1929 (International). Truck and car lines wouldn't receive separate identities until the production lines were separated—a process that wouldn't begin in earnest until 1934.

Technical upgrades continued throughout the 1920s. A modern dry-plate, disc-type clutch replaced the old cone-type unit in 1925. A stronger three-speed gearbox was introduced that year as well. In 1928 Chevrolet provided standard four-wheel brakes for both the half- and one-ton lines.

Body construction evolved in the 1920s, too. All truck cabs and beds seen before 1925 came from independent contractors. But, a little inspiration from Henry Ford once more helped change this situation.

Ford had begun marketing a pickup-style express body for its Model TT one-ton in October 1923. The company's first factory-built passenger compartment, an open C-cab, then followed in January 1924. Ford's first enclosed TT cab debuted in the spring of 1925 just about the time that Dearborn also was rolling out its Model T Runabout with Pick-Up Body. Again, Chevy's choice was made clear: keep up with the Joneses or else.

By then the company John and Horace Dodge had founded in 1914 (the two brothers both died in 1920) had already teamed up with Ray, Robert, and Joseph Graham to build factory-complete trucks. Beginning in 1921, Dodge Brothers delivered drivelines and other components to the Graham Brothers plant in Evansville, Indiana. There, Graham-designed and -built cabs and bodies were added, and these Graham-badged trucks were sold and serviced through Dodge dealerships right alongside the latter's commercial cars. Graham Brothers didn't officially become a division of Dodge Brothers until October 1924, the same year Dodge began marketing a factory-built (in Indiana) three-quarter-ton pickup complete with cab and body, both again supplied by Graham.

Chevrolet once more found itself last on a list. The division had been marketing more and more trucks with aftermarket bodywork installed right on the assembly line as the 1920s rolled on, but it wasn't the same. This process was by no means the most efficient, cost-conscious way to offer "complete-from-the-factory" trucks to customers. The extra expense of out-sourcing cabs and bodies still had to be passed on to buyers. Fortunately, Chevrolet did have an ace in the hole.

GM first contracted with the Fisher Body Company, founded by the six Fisher brothers in 1908, to manufacture Cadillac bodies in 1910. Between 1910 and 1919, the Fisher firm also supplied high-quality bodies

to many other auto makers, including Hudson, Chalmers, Studebaker, and Maxwell. Then, along came Billy Durant and his insatiable appetite for additional suppliers and supporters for his growing empire. The already-famous coach-builder was basically drawn into Durant's web after GM officials purchased 60 percent of the Fisher Body Corporation (the company had been reformed in 1916) in November 1919. GM snatched up the remaining 40 percent chunk of Fisher in June 1926, resulting in another reformation, this time into the Fisher Body Division of General Motors.

Although it had continued accepting orders from rival corporations, including Chrysler, up until that year, Fisher Body had been busy enough during the 1920s building bodies for the various GM divisions. Closed-bodies then were becoming all the rage, and it was this shape of things to come that represented Fisher's main claim to fame. So it was only natural that Fisher Body became the source when Chevrolet sought a way catch up to the commercial-vehicle competition.

According to *Automotive Industries*, on August 25, 1926, the Fisher body divisionannounced "the development of a distinct type of commercial body, built entirely within the organization for use on Chevrolet [truck] chassis." This closed cab, supplied by Fisher Body, featured plate-glass side windows with Ternstedt regulators and was intended only for one-ton trucks. Half-ton delivery models continued on as bare-chassis offerings from the factory. The tasks of completely outfitting a light truck and adding a bed or cargo box to a one-ton remained the sole responsibility of the aftermarket until 1930.

Bodywork from Martin-Parry, Hercules, and the rest remained popular even after Chevrolet began offering its own Fisher-built cabs in 1926. But anyone with eyes could see what the future held as the 1920s wound down. The independent coach-builder's days were numbered; soon both the car- and truck-making games would be played primarily in-house.

By 1930 no one was playing those games any harder than General Motors: not Chrysler, not even Ford. Though it had been somewhat slow in coming, the era of the modern pickup finally was at hand. And, as the 1920s came to a close, Chevrolet's pickup people stood ready to get a grip on this new market and not let go—not for another 30 years or so.

Real Steel

True Chevy Pickups Emerge

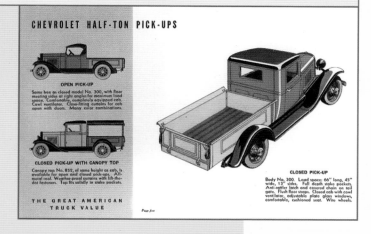

CHEVROLET HALF-TON PICK-UPS

OPEN PICK-UP

Same box as closed model No. 300, with floor meeting sides at right angles for maximum load space. Comfortable, completely equipped cab. Cowl ventilator. Close-fitting curtains for cab open with doors. Many color combinations.

CLOSED PICK-UP WITH CANOPY TOP

Canopy top No. 852, of same height as cab, is available for open and closed pick-ups. All-metal roof. Weather-proof curtains with lift-the-dot fasteners. Top fits solidly in stake pockets.

THE GREAT AMERICAN TRUCK VALUE

CLOSED PICK-UP

Body No. 300. Load space: 66" long, 45" wide, 13" sides. Full depth stake pockets. Anti-rattler latch and covered chain on tail gate. Flush floor straps. Closed cab with cowl ventilator, adjustable plate glass windows, comfortable, cushioned seat. Wire wheels.

Page five

Above

Simple bare-chassis models were replaced in the 1930s by a line of Chevrolet's own light trucks. The canopy express was a reasonably popular truck up until World War II. The 1932 pickups are depicted here.

Left

Chevrolet began selling factory-complete, steel-bodied half-ton pickups immediately after buying out the Martin-Parry body company in November 1930. By the time this 1932 Chevy was originally sold, the buyer no longer had to worry about shopping for additional components; complete bodywork was finally included in the factory price.

enry Ford built his fortune by making simple cars and selling them cheaply. Yet, with time Ford's stubborn devotion to simplicity created opportunities for his competitors. By the late 1920s, he still refused to update many aging features of his increasingly anti-quated products, and argued that simplicity was Ford's strongest selling point. Case in point was the transverse buggy spring, a relic of the horseless carriage days that continued to suspend Ford cars at both ends until 1949—only because Henry said so. He went on saying so long after Chevrolet introduced its inno-vative knee-action independent front suspension in 1934. "We use transverse springs for the same reason that we use round wheels," he huffed, "because we have found nothing better for the purpose."

Obviously superior modern advances, like hydraulic brakes and Hotchkiss drive, also failed to turn Henry's head. Chevrolet began installing hydraulic stoppers on its cars in 1935. Mechanical brakes continued offering Ford drivers "the safety of steel from toe to wheel" until 1939, again by the boss' iron-willed mandate. A Hotchkiss-type open driveshaft didn't replace Ford's enclosed torque-tube drive until Dearborn's modern postwar models finally arrived in 1949.

Chevrolet's model name for both car and truck lines in 1932 was "Confederate." A closed-cab Confederate pickup early that year carried a base price of $470. Economic woes inspired officials to lower that price to $440 later in 1932.

Like the Model T it had powered for so many years, Ford's diehard four-cylinder engine also was allowed to get a little too long in the tooth before Henry finally ordered a change. Before 1920, his mind had been typically made up. "I've got no use for a motor that has more spark plugs than a cow has teats," he once growled during the Model T's heyday. Nonetheless, as early as 1921, his engineers began work on a new engine with twice as many cylinders that would hopefully help Ford stay ahead of the competition. Not long afterward, the decision was made to roll out a suitable successor to the venerable Model T, which was finally retired in 1927.

Ford the man was still a god to the masses in the 1920s, although some citizens by 1925 had been heard complaining of the Ford car's "old-fashioned" nature. Model T sales weren't exactly suffering, but the man at least could have begun listening to constructive criticism earlier than he did. He also should have heard footsteps.

The much younger, hungrier Chevy was gaining more and more ground on its chief rival each year. Chevrolet had a head of steam up before Ford even had a fire lit under its pot full of ideas for the future.

The Model T's highly anticipated replacement, the Model A, surely would have served Henry better had it shown up a few years earlier. He didn't help matters much by completely closing down production in May 1927 to prepare for the Model A's epic introduction, which itself took its sweet time arriving. Some six months of idle assembly lines later, the historic 1928 Model A was unveiled to a wide-eye public on December 2. But critics' raves couldn't pay the bills, and Ford hadn't built a single car in a half a year.

At the same time, former Ford man William Knudsen was presiding over the sale of more than a million Chevys for 1927. Boom! For the first time in its

Above
A single-throat downdraft carburetor fed the 1932 Chevy's 194-ci six-cylinder. Compression was 5.2:1.

Left
As Chevy trucks did until 1936, the 1932 half-ton kept its gas tank underneath the seat. It was moved back underneath the bed four years later.

relatively short history, Chevrolet soared to the industry's top spot, a place the old veteran Ford had been famously familiar with for 20 years. Production-line problems in Dearborn allowed Chevrolet to top the charts with ease a second time in 1928 before the Model A got rolling and carried Ford back to first in 1929. From there, a tough battle ensued, as Chevrolet had its own history to make that year.

A December 1928 *Automobile Trade Journal* report called it "an epoch in motor car development." Company hype designated it "the outstanding Chevrolet of Chevrolet history." Nicknames included "Cast-Iron Wonder" and "Stovebolt." Introduced just before Thanksgiving in 1928, the object of all this affection and acclaim was Chevrolet's new six-cylinder engine. Not just any six, this was an overhead-valve six, a smooth, efficient powerplant that picked up where Chevy's tried-and-true OHV four-cylinder left off. Though various six-cylinder prototypes built prior to February 1927 all had been of the yeoman L-head design (or "side-valve"—the valves were in the block to the side of each cylinder), a more advanced OHV rendition represented the logical step up. After all, the well-worn company slogan had always been "valves in head, ahead in value."

Value remained a merit of Chevy's new OHV engine, so much so that a new slogan was also in order: "six in the price range of a four." Bottom lines for various 1929 six-cylinder models ranged only $10 to $30 higher than their four-cylinder forerunners from 1928. And for that extra dough, Chevrolet customers not only received two additional cylinders, they also took home 23 more cubic inches and 11 more horses. Rated at 46 horsepower, the 194-cid Stovebolt six was fed by a Carter one-barrel mounted in the then-typical updraft position.

Like that overhead-valve layout, the crank also qualified as "modern." Called a new development in the manufacture of six-cylinder crankshafts, this 46-pound single-plane forging was balanced both statically and dynamically. Unfortunately, it was only held in place by three main bearings, and it also handled the bulk of the lubrication chores by the age-old splash method. A less-than-stout bottom end represented the original Stovebolt's primary weakness.

Overall, however, the Chevy six was a real winner, a fact Henry Ford quickly discovered. William Knudsen

ordered his engineers to create the Cast-Iron Wonder once he learned that Ford had a new model in the works. Tit for tat. The engineers actually had that engine ready for 1928, but Knudsen chose to hold back and let the Model A have its day in the sun first. Meanwhile, his designers added four more inches to the wheelbases of Chevrolet's revamped National-series cars and trucks for 1928. A *MoTor* magazine review of the National line noted that every one of those inches had been added at the vehicles' noses—to make more room up there for two extra cylinders perhaps?

Knudsen rolled out his new Chevrolet Six about a year after the four-cylinder Model A first made headlines. Although the fresh Ford had its way in 1929 and 1930, it was the Stovebolt Chevy that reigned supreme in 1931 and again in 1932, even after Henry Ford made more history by introducing his "flathead" V-8. Who knows what might have happened had Henry's "eight-for-the-price-of-four" shown up a few years earlier along with the Model A. Once again, the old man's timing

HERCULES

Hercules No. 3993 All Steel Pick-Up Body
For 1931 Chevrolet Roadster Delivery
LOADING SPACE—Length 66″; Width 45″; Height of Side Panels 11½″.
Approximate Body Weight—Net 230 lbs. No Crating Required.
Finish—Blue.
CODE WORD: *Sylph.*

A Rugged Body, light in weight, and attractive in design, built of 1⅛-gauge special processed steel. Stake pockets, drop sides covering frame, corrugated bottom.

46   BETTER BUSINESS BODIES

The New Chevrolet Sedan Delivery

Proved Economy

Hardly a day goes by without some new and famous name being added to the long list of Chevrolet Six fleet owners. For, it is a matter of record among many large fleet operators that the Chevrolet Six is the most economical motor vehicle. A gasoline consumption of twenty miles to the gallon, or better, is not an unusual experience. Operators frequently comment on Chevrolet's unusual ability to keep running, day after day, without need for adjustment or repair. And speedometer readings on many Chevrolet cars still in active daily service show 50,000 miles or more. Naturally, when an automobile proves itself so economical in the service of large business firms, it represents an extremely wise investment as a personal car. Particularly so, when you consider what Chevrolet offers above and beyond economy—its modish Fisher Body style, its liberal comfort, its complete security, its smooth, alert, flexible six-cylinder performance.

Chevrolet passenger car prices range from $475 to $650. Chevrolet truck chassis are priced from $355 to $590. All prices f. o. b. Flint, Michigan. Special equipment extra. Low delivered prices and easy terms. Chevrolet Motor Company, Detroit, Michigan.

NEW CHEVROLET SIX

looked a bit off. Throw in some major teething problems and a Depression-riddled economy, and it was little wonder that those V-8 Fords failed to catch the Chevy Sixes in 1932 or 1933.

Results differed slightly on the truck side of the fence, undoubtedly due to Ford's head start in the pickup race. Like their car-line cousins, Chevrolet commercial vehicles took advantage of Dearborn's downtime in 1927 and rose to the top for the first time. They were America's best-selling trucks again in 1928 before Ford regained the lead and held it for four straight years. Chevy's Cast-Iron Wonder apparently wasn't as wonderful on the truck side. In truth, the situation had nothing to do with the new

engine's merits. No way was Ford's L-head four a better choice then Chevy's OHV six in a car or a truck.

The Chevrolet Six boasted ample power, excellent gas mileage, smooth operation, and unquestioned dependability, all at a low, low price. How could it get any better? "Hardly a day goes by without some new and famous name being added to the long list of Chevrolet Six fleet owners," began a 1931 ad touting "The Great American Value." "For it is a matter of record among many large fleet operators that the Chevrolet Six is the most economical motor vehicle. A gasoline consumption of 20 miles to the gallon, or better, is not an unusual experience. Operators frequently comment on Chevrolet's unusual ability to keep running, day after day, without need for adjustment or repair."

That Ford's four-cylinder trucks held on to first place in the early-1930s while its cars fell to second was due to the changing face of the commercial vehicle market. The American pickup we all know today really got rolling after 1930, with light trucks making up more and more of the market each proceeding year. It was no coincidence that so many companies had begun building pickups by 1936; the market's lightest segment had become the most lucrative almost overnight. This time Henry Ford's timing couldn't have been any better.

Before 1929, Ford was basically alone in the pickup field. It was the only company in America offering a true factory-complete, all-steel half-ton. Though it was a modified Model T roadster, Ford's earliest light truck still deserved the honor of being this country's first pickup and understandably remained the most popular for many years. That popularity began looming even larger after an enclosed cab was introduced for the new Model A chassis in 1928. Ford continued building roadster pickups until 1934. But the weather-proof, full-roofed half-ton naturally became the main choice immediately after its arrival. Production of closed-cab Model A pickups in 1929 soared to nearly 78,000. Another 86,000 followed in 1930, and 98,000 hit the road in 1931—all still powered by Henry's good ol' four-banger.

Walter P. Chrysler made sure his newly purchased Dodge truck division officially joined the pickup fraternity in 1929. As for Chevrolet, in this case it was Knudsen's decision-makers who were hesitant.

Chevy's new International-series truck line (now rolling on standard steel-disc wheels) shifted gears too in 1929, but upward, as the one-ton models were dropped in favor of truly tough one-and-one-half-ton haulers. Half-ton chassis, some even crowned with Chevy-built enclosed cabs right on a Chevrolet assembly line, remained the company's lightest offerings. Pickup bodies (i.e., cargo boxes) were still the responsibility of the aftermarket in 1929, and some of these out-sourced options were installed by Chevrolet too. Martin-Parry, Hercules, and the rest continued printing up catalogs full of add-on bodies and cabs for Chevrolet trucks into 1930 only because GM simply hadn't yet committed itself to the full production of a real pickup—that is, a real steel pickup fully fitted with a cab and box designed, manufactured, and sold complete by Chevrolet, not a co-op deal involving an independent contractor.

Ford's closed-cab Model A half-ton in 1928 set another standard: no more converted roadsters. Although slipping out-sourced cargo boxes into the trunks of Chevrolet automobiles had been a neat trick in the 1920s, the resulting truly light utility vehicle never could compete with Ford's Model T trucks. Nor did a "real" roadster pickup (one with a true pickup body

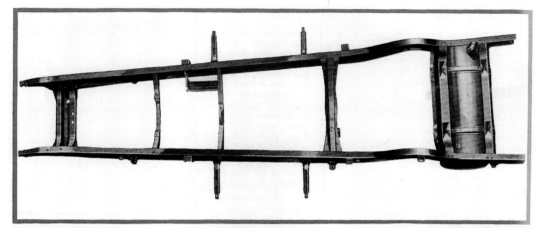

THE HALF-TON FRAME

The half-ton truck has a rugged, full length frame which is 164 inches long. The channel steel side members are 5¾ inches deep with 2¼-inch flanges. Five strong cross members provide rigid support. This frame gives the large capacity Chevrolet truck bodies adequate support as it extends well beyond the center line of the rear axle. The rear cross member protects the 16-gallon gasoline tank. A gasoline filler cap is located on right-hand side of all Chevrolet bodies and it is conveniently placed for filling. The illustration at the right shows the efficient load distribution. The center of the load is 3⅞ inches ahead of the center line of the rear axle.

16

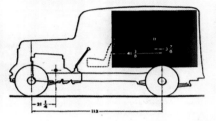

in back instead of that box-in-a-trunk) comparable to the Model T runabout have a chance of carrying the day after closed pickups from both Ford and Dodge appeared in 1929.

Nonetheless, Chevrolet did try the open pickup route, and introduced its Roadster Delivery half-ton late in 1928. This vehicle's radiator shell, hood panels, cowl, and doors were all taken from Chevy's convertible passenger-car. Able to both flip down and swing out, the windshield was two inches taller than the car-line roadster's, and the pickup's canvas top was stretched over a removable rigid frame made of wood and steel. Completing the deal was a back wall added behind the seat to form a cab. Fenders and running boards were also typically included, but the pickup box was left up to the customer to install. The base price (without the box) was about $515.

Although very attractive, Chevrolet's Roadster Delivery pickup represented old news by the time it made the scene, explaining why this sporty little truck was only offered up through 1932. As it was, Chevy officials had good reason to give up on their topless pickup two years before Ford. They had something better. Finally.

Hercules was still building bodies for Chevy truck chassis in 1932, but the Martin-Parry connection had

A stronger, longer frame was also new for the 1934 Chevrolet pickup, which featured a 4,400-pound gross vehicle weight rating. That figure had been 4,100 pounds in 1933.

1930s Rivals

Pickin' Up The Pace

International-Harvester joined the pickup race late in 1932 by way of a contract deal with Willys-Overland. Willys supplied International with its C-series pickup, and International simply rebadged it as its D-1 light truck.

Willys had been a player in the light-truck field throughout the 1930s and then produced one of the classiest-looking pickups of the pre-war era in 1941.

By 1930 each of the Big Three truck divisions was offering a true pickup. A factory-complete, all-steel, half-ton truck. Buoyed by this new breed's popularity, Ford, Chevrolet, and Dodge finished, in that order, far ahead of the rest of the commercial vehicle field in that year's sales race. Eighty-one percent of the market in 1930 belonged to the Big Three, and that percentage rose another two points if GMC, 1930's fourth best-selling truck, was included.

The other 17 percent of the 1930 truck pie was left to a rambling collection of independent manufacturers—some famous, and the other not so famous. International, Reo, Mack, and Studebaker were among the former, and the latter group included the likes of Moreland, Relay, Rugby, and Schact. Medium- and heavy-duty machines represented the main claims to fame for nearly all of these companies. That reality soon changed thanks to the emergence of the traditional half-ton truck. Everyone seemed to play the pickup game as the decade wound down.

The Depression played a role in the pickup's ever-growing prominence. Low sales influenced more than one big-truck builder in the early 1930s to search out a savior and sell something easier than the high-priced, hulking pack mules that previously hauled their bread and butter. The low-priced, lightweight commercial vehicle was the obvious choice in the minds of International-Harvester executives in Chicago. Their decision to market a pickup came so fast there wasn't enough time for I-H to create one itself. Late in 1932, International-Harvester simply turned to its counterparts at Willys-Overland, who had introduced its own half-ton truck the year before. A deal was made whereby I-H's plant in Toledo, Ohio, would rebadge the Willys half-ton and trade its four-cylinder engine for a six. The result was International's first pickup, the D-1. It debuted in January 1933, just in time to help boost I-H's sales for the year by 70 percent.

A boost to Depression-riddled sales was undoubtedly the goal at Stewart and Reo, two long-standing commercial vehicle manufacturers that had toyed with half-tons in the 1920s before they became serious in the 1930s. Results differed greatly, however. The half-ton Buddy Stewart couldn't quite carry the load, and its parent company was out of business by 1942.

Reo, on the other hand, was more firmly rooted, thanks in part to the fact that it built cars and trucks. In the summer of 1936, Reo officials announced they would end the 31-year-old automotive legacy immediately to concentrate on commercial vehicles. The company, originally founded by Ransom E. Olds, did well with its half-ton Speed Delivery pickups during the 1930s, and is still known for its Speed Wagon trucks. Unlike Stewart, Reo returned to the truck market after the war, but never built another light-duty pickup. Reo's one-ton D-19X truck didn't exactly qualify as "light-duty."

Studebaker had also dabbled in big trucks prior to 1930. The veteran Indiana concern unveiled its first pickup in 1937. Like Reo's earliest half-tons, Studebaker's new light-truck was a converted automobile. From the doors forward, the 1937 Coupe Express was a Studebaker Dictator passenger car, an attractive hybrid that reminded many witnesses of Hudson's Terraplane pickup that was introduced three years earlier. Hudson continued to offer its "half-car, half-truck" until 1947. Studebaker built its variety for three years before it rolled out an "all-pickup" pickup in 1940.

Plymouth gave Chrysler Corporation a second pickup line in 1937. Like Reo's half-ton Speed Wagons, these "dressed-down" Dodge half-tons didn't survive the war. The American Bantam's little pint-sized pickups, which ran from 1929 (known then as American Austin) to

1941, also suffered the same fate. Crosley's tiny quarter-ton truck debuted late in 1939 as a 1940 model, and picked up where the Bantam left off. Crosley pickups did reappear after World War II, but they barely lasted into the 1950s. Americans at the time apparently weren't ready for compact trucks, but big-rig builders back in the 1930s certainly had nothing against smaller trucks. Federal, Diamond T, and Mack each tried to downsize into the pickup field as a way to boost sales after the Depression had done its worst.

Federal founder Martin Pulcher announced his company's first pickup, the Model 10, in December 1935. Offered in three-quarter- and one-ton forms, the Model 10 filled a perceived gap in the truck market. Some light, bulky loads were too much for the typical half-ton, yet not heavy enough for a one-and-one-half-tonner to handle efficiently, a situation Pulcher hoped would inspire a demand for his "light-heavyweight" pickups. That demand never really did take off, although Federal continued to offer a big pickup up through 1950.

Diamond T in Chicago also tried the big pickup route and began with its three-quarter-ton Model 80 truck in 1936. This stylish machine was superseded two years later by the classic Model 201 one-ton, "a unique vehicle in the light-duty field" according to factory brochures. "Its all-truck specifications and exceptionally rugged construction set it widely apart from most trucks in this classification because they are commonly passenger car adaptations, which include the use of many units originally designed for passenger car service." After about 7,000 (most were painted red) were built, the Model 201 was replaced in 1950 by the bare-chassis, one-ton Model 222, Diamond T's last stab at the light-duty field.

Contrary to Diamond T's purpose-built pickups, Mack's first light-trucks were passenger car adaptations, and that was a neat trick since the company never built automobiles. Mack officials looked outside their facilities when the time came to expand downward into the pickup field. Mack called up Reo late in 1934 and asked to badge-engineer its car-based Speed Delivery truck into a new Mack product. A different grille, appropriate emblems, and the world-famous bulldog mascot were added, and presto: Reo's light-truck became the Mack Jr. Built from 1936 to 1938, the Mack Jr (no period was used in official descriptions) pickup was offered with four- or six-cylinder power, and in half- or three-quarter-ton form.

Many Mack-watchers have since speculated that the light Reo-based trucks were rushed to market as a quick-fix until the company could engineer a pickup of its own comparable to the Diamond T 201. That vehicle, the Model ED one-ton, did appear in 1938 and was every bit as purposeful as Diamond T's light-heavyweight.

"Here is no makeshift attempt to build up a lighter model or build down a heavier one," Mack brochures stated. "Uniformly rugged and perfectly proportioned throughout, Model ED is literally a small-scale, heavy-duty truck." Mack built its rugged ED up through 1944, and all models manufactured after 1941 went to the U.S. military for use as fire-fighting equipment. The legendary big-rig builder then left the light-duty field to the lightweights. Beginning in 1946, it was business as usual for the Big Three with only International and Studebaker pestering Detroit with rival pickups after 1950.

Big-rig builder Diamond T introduced its Model 80 pickup midyear in 1936. Like nearly all Diamond T pickups, this 1937 Model 80 sports the trademark red paint and green pinstriping.

Studebaker, too, simply modified a passenger-car model into its first pickup, called the Coupe Express. Introduced in 1937, the Coupe Express was built for three years. These are 1938 models.

Like International, Mack looked to an outside contractor for help competing in the light truck market. Thus, it was REO that supplied its car-based half-ton truck to Mack, which rebadged it as the Mack Jr. This is a 1937 half-ton Mack Jr.—three-quarter-ton versions were also built.

Far left
Both first- and second-series pickups were built in 1936, with the latter appearing here. Second-series trucks featured Chevrolet's first all-steel cab and a lower roofline compared to the first-series models. This 1936 second-series half-ton also sports mysterious dual sidemount spares, perhaps resulting long ago from the mixing and matching of GMC and Chevy fenders. The two corporate cousins normally installed their single sidemounts on opposite sides.

Left
First-series Chevrolet trucks in 1936 still used a separate roof panel on top. GM's innovative "turret-top" stampings, first shown off on Chevy cars in 1935, made the lower, more rakish all-steel cab possible the following year.

ended two years before, because GM had bought out the Indianapolis firm in November 1930, giving Chevrolet the ability to manufacture all its own bodywork. The division's first fully enclosed factory-complete half-ton, politely priced at $440, followed immediately. By 1931 the Big Three pickup race was on.

Chevrolet truck sales, now fueled by the ever-increasing popularity of the pickup, began gathering serious steam in the 1930s. It had taken the company 11 years to build its first 500,000 commercial vehicles. The second half-million rolled out over the next four years, helping Chevrolet to again become America's best-selling truck in 1933. Ford led briefly in 1935 and 1937, and then there was no looking back. Chevrolet's one millionth truck appeared 15 years after its first. A

mere six years elapsed before the two millionth rolled out the door in 1939. Ads that year summed it all up simply enough: "Chevrolet is the nation's largest builder of trucks because buyers of single trucks and buyers of large fleets both agree that it pays in all ways to buy Chevrolets!' "

Sales climbed so drastically during the 1930s because the trucks improved by leaps and bounds. The decade had begun with Chevrolet not even in the pick-up business. It ended with the company building the best pickups by the boatload. And good luck had nothing to do with that success. Once GM's low-priced division began pickup production, it did so with a purpose. Unlike Henry Ford, Chevy's truck builders didn't give a spit about the past; they embraced the future every bit as

firmly as their co-workers on the car line—perhaps even tighter, considering how far the Chevrolet pickup advanced from 1930 to 1940.

Truck line upgrades were plentiful each year, beginning with a warmly welcomed wider cab with bigger doors for the new Independence line introduced for 1931. Anyone who has driven a Chevy truck from the 1920s can attest to the fact that these vehicles were not built for big boys. No way, no how. Entering and exiting was best left to contortionists. And once inside, there was barely enough room left-to-right for a driver and his broad-shouldered buddy—man's true best friend usually had to wag his tail in back. Increased cab dimensions (the seat was widened, too) in 1931 helped this cramped situation some, though all pickup cabs were still confining at best.

Another improvement for the Independence-series cab involved the addition of a one-piece steel roof in place of the wood-framed, fabric-covered concoction used previously to keep riders close and dry inside. Calling early pickups "all-steel" is an over-simplification, a word-economizer chosen to mark the departure from the all-wood construction common to all truck cabs and bodies before 1920. While Ford's progenitor of the pickup breed did feature a steel cab and body in 1925, the cab was composed of steel sheathing surrounding a wooden frame. All "all-steel" pickups, including Chevrolet's, were built this way into the 1930s because that was the limit of the technology then. But the use of wood framing diminished each year. "All-steel" really meant all steel, without wooden chassis members, by 1936—at least in Chevy pickup terms.

Chevrolet's commercial vehicles got the lead on their automotive counterparts, for once, in departing from partial wood construction. Independence-series closed truck cabs in 1931 incorporated an all-steel cowl, called a "commercial cowl." Cowls in Independence-series cars (and thus those on roadster pickups too) that year continued to use steel-on-wood construction. This meant that pickup doors were more durably hinged on an all-steel post, as opposed to a wooden post simply covered in steel. Wood disappeared completely from Chevy pickup cabs midyear in 1936.

When the Confederate series was introduced in 1932, both cars and trucks gained extra durability from

front bracing called the Stabilizer Unit. Brochures explained that the front fenders, radiator, and headlamps were all mounted as a unit: "This construction eliminates excessive movements of these parts, protects the radiator core, prevents rattles and squeaks, and makes driving on rough roads easier." And it was rough roads that separated the men from the boys—or trucks from cars.

Advances made during the 1930s also helped redefine the half-ton pickup as a full-fledged truck, not just a modified car. When the decade began, Chevrolet cars and pickups were all but identical up front, sharing nearly all frontal body components. Those family ties first started coming undone in 1932, as the car line's face was freshened, while that year's new light trucks continued wearing the previous year's front sheet metal. Leftover year-old car styling was again featured on 1933's trucks, which were the last new commercial models introduced with the same series name as their automotive cousins. In this case, the label was Master Eagle, or just Eagle.

The Suburban | *A Sporting Proposition*

Easily the longest running legacy in the utility vehicle is Chevrolet's Suburban, born rather humbly in 1935. All Suburbans were two-door models until 1973.

The truck market's meteoric rise to prominence during the last decade or so can be attributed to the emergence of two variations on the utility-vehicle theme: the minivan and the SUV. The minivan burst onto the scene in the late 1980s, and then peaked in the early 1990s. While minivans remain quite popular today, they're almost lost in the shadow of the SUV. The supposedly safer "sport-ute" has brought buyers in ever-increasing numbers, and has also stolen them away from other once-popular market segments such as the two-door sport coupe. Ford gave up on its Thunderbird in 1997, and GM stands ready to do the same with its long-running F-body (Camaro/Firebird) platform, both thanks to the sport-utility vehicle's ravenous appetite for the entire four-wheeled industry.

As Ford public affairs person Jim Bright explained in 1997 in response to the T-bird's demise, "two-door coupes used to be familiar to family types in the market for utility and versatility, but a greater number of customers are now turning to light-trucks instead of cars." Fortunately for Ford, the Mustang continues to gallop along and will soon have the once-packed pony car field all to itself after Chevrolet and Pontiac bow out after 35 years. How long that field will remain fertile is anyone's guess.

General Motors was the first outstanding player in the SUV field, although Ford cultivated the lead in 1997. Dearborn can never take away the fact that Chevrolet originally planted the sport-ute seeds. While the bulk of the breed's growth has come during the last 20 years or so, the roots of the concept date back more than a half-century.

Chevrolet's Suburban, by far the oldest member of the SUV family, was introduced in 1935 at a time when trucks and cars existed on opposite sides of the transportation market fence. The thought of cars and trucks sharing America's load was unthinkable then, and rightly so considering how comparatively crude and singularly focused the "manly" light-truck was at the time. Getting in touch with the pickup's feminine side was even more inconceivable 65 years ago.

That's not to say, however, that the idea of a multi-role vehicle that incorporated the best of both worlds was entirely new in 1935. Young and inexperienced, the station wagon could carry passengers and cargo equally well and fit in just as nicely on the farm or in town, but these were cars that were limited by their car-line capabilities. On top of that, nearly all early station wagons were the custom-built products of aftermarket body suppliers. When nearly all of the pickups were fitted with all-steel cabs and beds, the pioneering wagons of the early 1930s required a carpenter to nail the bodies together. Thus the endearing nickname that remains well-known to this day: "woody."

When the "Carryall Suburban" debuted in 1935, it was dubbed the industry's first all-steel "station wagon" even though it was marketed as part of Chevy's upscale Master truck line. While it looked very much like a car up front, it featured a half-ton pickup chassis underneath, which meant its load capacity was superior to any station wagon's.

As many as eight people could ride comfortably in the first Suburban. This progenitor of today's practical people-mover could be stripped of its two rear seats to make room for a truckload of cargo. With the two rear seats removed, the cargo bay measured 52 inches wide by 75 inches long.

The removable passenger seats helped set the Suburban apart from Chevrolet's yeoman sedan delivery that was introduced in 1928. Most noticeable, however, was the

Today's Suburban is bigger, classier and more comfortable than ever, and can still carry its own weight when it has too. Here an 1988 K2500 4x4 Suburban tows one of its ancestors, a 1946 Suburban.

GMC has also marketed a Suburban model since the 1930s. Flashier grilles set GMC trucks apart from their less prestigious Chevrolet cousins in the 1950s. Shown here is a 1957 GMC Suburban.

1935 Suburban's airy side glass in place of the sedan delivery's solid-steel walls. Passengers could take in the sights in pleasant fashion during their trip. The Carryall Suburban, in Chevrolet's words, combined "the advantages of a passenger car and a light delivery unit." Brochures claimed: "As you desire it, this all-purpose vehicle serves you in business or in pleasure."

When this all-purpose machine first made the scene in 1935, such claims made headlines. Even so, apparently the rest of Detroit was slow to take notice. Other than GMC's Suburban, no other knock-offs appeared in the 1930s. Although Willys-Overland did introduce a similar truck-based station wagon in 1946, it wasn't until International-Harvester rolled out its attractive Travelall in 1956 that a true direct competitor emerged.

Willys' reformed successor, Kaiser-Jeep, redirected that competition in 1963 with the creation of its Wagoneer, a stylish, classy, and tough utility vehicle that may qualify as the "father of the modern SUV." Two years before, International had also put a new twist to sport-ute pre-history when the Scout, America's first fun-to-drive, off-road, multi-role pickup, was introduced. Ford followed suit in 1966 with its first Bronco, which was offered as a full-roofed wagon, a roadster pickup with a soft-top, or a roadster pickup with a removable hardtop. The last version was given its own unique name: "Sports Utility."

Chevrolet responded with the Blazer in 1969. Chevy labelmakers three years later also added another piece to the SUV puzzle when it named its new mini-pickup. "LUV" wasn't just a cute calling card in 1972, it was technically short for "light-utility vehicle." A decade later, "SUV" evolved into the generic reference for all of the light-truck variations.

A new two-piece windshield on Chevrolet's roomier 1939 truck cab replaced the one-piece glass used in 1938. The grille layout was also more distinctive.

The Master-series reference faded away on the truck side as the decade rolled on.

Trucks and cars finally parted ways big-time in 1934, when pickups were first treated to their own individualistic styling. That grille and radiator shell on your 1934 Chevy half-ton may have looked like the setup seen on that year's new automobile, but none of the pair's main body components interchanged. Although certain styling elements were shared during the next few years, Chevrolet pickups would never again look like a Chevy car with a cargo box bolted on in back.

Compared to its boxy, rather simple forerunners, Chevrolet's restyled 1934 pickup certainly looked modern. Softer lines and corners were now rounded instead of squared off, and the windshield was canted rearward ever so slightly. But "gangly" was still a fair description, thanks to that tall cab, an old-style passenger compartment that appeared to look even taller than it really was because of its relatively tight width.

That impression was further modernized in 1936. As they would again in 1947 and 1955, Chevrolet truck builders chose to start that year carrying over the previous year's design, resulting in "first-series" and "second-series" models. Chevy fans know these two more personally as the "high-roof" and "low-roof," respectively,

because the second series featured a restyled, much more rakish cab that was noticeably shorter. First-series 1936 cabs were 53-3/4 inches tall, while their second-series successors measured 50-11/16 inches from roof to floor—which no longer included wood in its construction. The sleek, stylish second-series passenger compartment was Chevrolet's first honestly all-steel pickup cab.

It was also the truck line's first one-piece "turret-top" cab, an innovative design originally shown off on 1935 Chevy cars. Turret-top stampings did away with the separate roof panel required on all cabs prior to 1936. Along with being better looking, this one-piece construction also improved comfort and durability, virtues that all truck makers at the time were striving to heighten, broaden, strengthen—and promote.

Chevrolet officials were so proud of their latest, greatest trucks in 1936, they teamed up with the American Automobile Association late that year to pull off a stunt that hopefully would prove just how many ways their pickups were better than the competition's. On December 13, 1936, a 1937 Chevy half-ton driven by race driver Harry Hartz set out from Detroit on an AAA-sanctioned "Safe Driving Road Test" encompassing the rim of the United States. That is, the course would run west across the upper states, down the West Coast, back

east across the southern regions, up the East Coast, and back west to Detroit. More than 10,000 miles were predicted. And to make things even more interesting, a 1,060-pound load was tossed in the back for good measure.

"The dependability and economy of a motor truck can best by proved by putting it through a grueling, arduous test under every type of operating condition," began a 1937 Chevrolet brochure detailing this epic voyage. "High-flung mountains, parched deserts, wind-swept fog, knee-deep mud, gale-whipped snow—nature's whole bag of tricks—had to be met time and again. Daily, the truck met and took in its stride every kind of road, weather, and punishment."

That Chevy pickup never missed a beat while travelling 10,244.8 miles over a two-month span. By the time it returned to Detroit on February 23, 1937, Hartz had spent only 73 cents on repair parts. He had averaged

31.18 miles per hour and 20.74 miles per gallon for the trip, translating into a fuel cost of less than one cent per mile. And Chevrolet had proved its point: "More Power per Gallon—Lower Cost per Load" wasn't just the latest truck slogan, it was the plain penny-pinching truth. It clearly did pay to buy a Chevrolet.

The Chevrolet that Hartz drove around (all the way around) America that winter was as good as it got in the pickup field up to that point. Not only great-looking—a rakish nose was paired up with 1936's second-series cab—Chevy's 1937 half-ton was just as modern beneath that trendy sheet metal thanks to its state-of-the-art hydraulic brakes, also introduced midyear in 1936. Equally notable was its new, modernized power source, Chevrolet's latest variation on its tried-and-true Stovebolt theme.

Initial variations in the powerplant had come five years before, when the truck line was treated to its first

Modern sealed-beam headlights became standard equipment for the 1940 Chevy pickup. Other updates that year included a revised instrument panel inside.

51

1936–1942 Coupe Pickups

Have Bed. Will Travel.

Chevrolet's first coupe-pickup debuted in 1936. The spare tire was moved to a sidemount position in the fender to make room in back for cargo.

All of Chevrolet's early light-trucks were nothing more than beefed-up cars, and some were beefed-up more than others. That situation began to change in a big way once Chevy pickups received sheet-metal of their own in 1934. After that, light-trucks looked like trucks, while cars continued to look like cars. Things were not always what they seemed, however. Sometimes a car looked like a car, but worked almost like a truck.

Such was the case in 1936 when Chevrolet introduced its "coupe pick-up." A clever combination of stylish passenger-car comfort with a little light-truck practicality, this intriguing new model was simply a Standard two-door business coupe with a cargo box mounted in the trunk. The trunk lid could be removed, and a mini-bed complete with a chain-locked pickup-style tailgate, could be inserted. The box's sidewalls were 12.25 inches high and the length from the upper lip of the existing trunk opening back to the tailgate was 41.5 inches. Total bed-floor length was 60 inches. Step pads were added to each end of the rear bumper to aid loading, and the spare tire was moved from its standard location within the trunk to a special sidemount right front fender.

"Here's a speedy, smart pick-up of surprisingly large capacity, which you can load and unload in a twinkling," bragged perky brochures in 1936. "Exceptionally economical on gas, oil, and tires, and ruggedly built to withstand grueling service" were among additional merits, although that "ruggedly built" comment could have been questioned. Except for the sidemount spare and pickup box in the trunk, everything else about the 1936 coupe pick-up was pure Chevrolet automobile, a fact those same brochures quietly admitted before closing: "It is a Standard passenger car adapted for commercial use." No ifs, ands, or buts about it.

If this supposedly new idea appeared familiar, it should have. More than one aftermarket body-builder had offered a similar conversion for Chevrolet coupes and roadsters during the 1920s, and this "slip-in box" conversion was still around in the early 1930s. By 1926, Chevrolet offered this combination in roadster form direct from the factory. The appearance of a true roadster pickup with a full cargo box instead of that slip-in unit in 1929 diminished the demand for these cars-converted-into-trucks. Although the demand was not enough that the theme couldn't experience a rebirth—in coupe-only form—in 1936.

This encore of an idea then apparently looked so good that various rivals couldn't resist jumping on the bandwagon. Plymouth and Chevrolet offered coupe-pickups that first year, Hudson and Ford joined them in 1937, and Studebaker joined in 1940. Chevrolet created the best example that ran for the longest amount of time. Ford and Studebaker's renditions were one-hit wonders, and Plymouth's apparently disappeared after 1939. Hudson's survived into the 1940s, but it was always overshadowed by its classy car-based pickups that turned heads from 1934 to 1947.

Chevrolet, meanwhile, continued to offer its car-with-a-pickup-box-in-its-trunk up until World War II shut down civilian automobile production early in 1942. Production ended with reasonable success considering this hybrid's limited appeal. It was no coincidence that Ford's coupe-pickup was on the market only for one year, and Studebaker's basically appeared just to temporarily bridge the gap between South Bend's Hudson-like, car-based Coupe-Express pickups of 1937–1939, and its first true half-ton truck, the M5, that rolled out of Indiana in 1941.

Chevrolet sold 3,183 coupe pick-ups in 1936 and still turned them out at a relatively "healthy" rate (1,135) in 1941. Only 206 were built during the brief 1942 model run. The longer, restyled Master business coupe became the base in 1937, and its stretched wheelbase (112.25 inches, compared to 1936's 109 inches) meant for a longer cargo box: 66.125 inches. The spare was relocated to a lockable compartment just below the tailgate, and the standard rear deck lid was also included to reconvert the 1937 pickup with a removable box back into a conventional business coupe at the owner's whim.

Coupe pickups basically carried on in this same form up through 1942. The only notable change occurred in 1940 when this curious concoction was offered both on the base Master 85 passenger-car chassis and the more refined (modernized knee-action front suspension was standard) Master Deluxe platform, with the latter available by special order only. Chevy's "top-shelf" Master Deluxe business coupe became the only choice for buyers who wanted the coupe pick-up conversion during the final two model runs.

Chevrolet's coupe pickup did not return after World War II, and it was probably the product of the final natural segregation of car and truck lines rather than the concession to marker pressures. Pickups had widened the utility vehicle's scope so far that there was no longer the need to pretend that a car could be a truck. Cars had their own world and simply didn't belong in the truck's world. A new breed of postwar pickup soon made the utility world a kinder, gentler place to live, work, and play. That place progressively began to look more and more like cars. Today it's the trucks that pretend to be cars.

Like Ford, Hudson, and Studebaker, Plymouth also offered a box-in-the-trunk option, with this particular model arriving in 1939.

COUPE PICK-UP

On Master 85 passenger car chassis . . . May be had with Knee-Action at additional cost . . . Body same as Master 85 Business Coupe with pick-up box added . . . Rear deck lid is furnished for converting into a business coupe . . . Pick-up box has tubular reinforcement of sides, and strong tail-gate. (See Page 31.)

Of the various converted business coupe/pickups built before World War II, Chevrolet's was the most successful. Chevy's coupe-pickup was offered from 1936 to 1942. Shown here is the 1940 rendition.

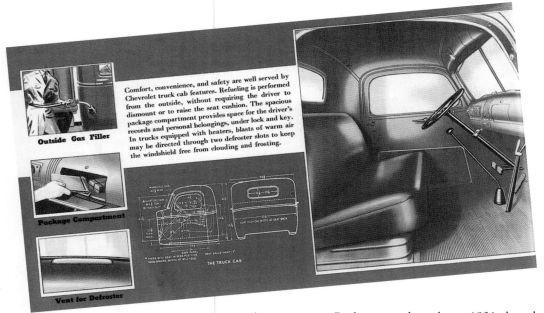

Comfort, convenience, and safety are well served by Chevrolet truck cab features. Refueling is performed from the outside, without requiring the driver to dismount or to raise the seat cushion. The spacious package compartment provides space for the driver's records and personal belongings, under lock and key. In trucks equipped with heaters, blasts of warm air may be directed through two defroster slots to keep the windshield free from clouding and frosting.

Outside Gas Filler

Package Compartment

Vent for Defroster

THE TRUCK CAB

Improving comfort by enlarging the cab was a top priority for Chevrolet truck designers during the years prior to World War II. A wheelbase stretch in 1939 allowed the introduction of a longer, wider, taller cab for that year's pickup. Brochures in 1940 touted that cab's many merits.

exclusive engine. Both cars and trucks in 1931 shared the same six-cylinder, then rated at 50 horsepower. In 1932, Chevrolet cars received an even stronger 60-horse six, while the trucks got a 53-horsepower version better suited for higher torque at lower rpm. Improved pulling power was the goal. Most noticeable among changes made was the downdraft carburetor that replaced the updraft unit.

New as well in 1932 was the "Silent Synchromesh" three-speed transmission bolted up in place of the antiquated spur-type three-speed used in 1931. The advent of the synchromesh gearbox meant an end to double-clutching—the left-leg workout well known to all truck drivers (and many car drivers, too) who lived with loud, cranky, non-synchronized trannies everyday. "If you can't find 'em, grind 'em," said it all about gear-jamming back then.

Chevy truck engine displacement increased to 207 cubic inches in 1933, with a corresponding output jump to 56 horsepower. Engineers had raised displacement from 194 cubes by stretching the stroke to four inches. Long-stroke engines are generally more economical and more torquey than short-strokers. But the latter type winds up higher and easier and creates more horsepower.

When those ever-present engineers put together a longer, stronger frame for the 1934 Chevy pickup, they built in strength and room for more powerful engines

and larger load capacities in the future. Representing another departure from those car-based roots, this more rugged, heavier platform helped increase the 1934 light-truck's gross-vehicle-weight rating from 4,100 pounds to 4,400. Wheelbase went up three inches to 112. The stage was then set for the appearance of an even mightier Stovebolt.

Increased compression and an improved cylinder head helped boost output to 68.5 horsepower in 1935. Another compression increase to 6.0:1 lifted horsepower again to 79 in 1936. Then came 1937. The long-running Stovebolt six experienced two major redesigns during its 34-year tenure. The first was performed only eight years after its introduction.

Chevy's six-cylinder was rebuilt for 1937 with an eye towards increasing both durability and power potential. The cylinder block was recast with extra length. Deck height, on the other hand, was shortened two inches. That last change went hand in hand with a rev-enhancing, shorter stroke, while the lengthened cylinder block made extra room for both bigger bores and an additional main bearing. Four main bearings were certainly better than three for holding things together during hard usage, especially considering that the engines still used an obsolete low-pressure oiling system and poured Babbitt bearings.

Even though the stroke was shortened from 4 to 3-3/4 inches, displacement increased to 216.5 cubes thanks to those bigger bores—3-1/2 inches compared to 3-5/16. Compression also rose to 6.25:1. The car-line version of this new six produced 85 horses; heavier, stronger pistons in the truck's six resulted in a lower rating of 78 horsepower. Not to worry, though; increasing that number in the future was to be no big deal.

Additional pickup upgrades in 1937 included a longer cargo box and two new midyear models, a three-quarter-ton and a one-ton. These two heavier light-trucks were suspended on a 122-1/4-inch wheelbase. Various chassis components were naturally heavier, too. An even longer, wider half-ton cargo box was bolted on in 1940, but more notable were the cab progressions seen just prior to World War II.

Increasing comfort, safety and convenience had been major priorities, too, during those prewar years. Making trucks safer to drive was mostly a matter of making sure the driver could both see out of the cab and stop his vehicle within reasonable distances.

Non-glare windshields first appeared on Chevy cars and trucks in 1930. Total glass area increased over the years, and by 1939 it measured 188 square inches, with the windshield now a trendy V-type split into two pieces that cranked out for extra ventilation. All windows were switched to safety-pane glass the following year. (Previous cabs had featured safety-glass windshields only.) Keeping that windshield clear was important as well. To that end, a vacuum-activated windshield wiper replaced the old hand-operated unit in 1930. A driver-side-only wiper remained standard before World War II, but at least the motor itself was recessed flush with the windshield header and fitted with knurled knobs in 1938 to make it less threatening to the driver's forehead.

Before Chevy pickups were fitted with modern four-wheel hydraulic brakes in mid 1936, those early mechanical stoppers had been improved with wider, longer linings in 1933. Linings were then changed to a new material (with a higher friction coefficient) two years later.

Cab improvements included redesigned seat cushions and backs for greater durability and comfort in 1938. Adding even more comfort was the goal when the Chevy pickup's wheelbase was stretched to 113.5 inches in 1939. This extra length allowed the installation of a new, roomier cab that remained in place with only a few minor modifications for eight years. In its earliest form, it measured 1-1/2 inches longer, 1-1/4 inches wider, and 1-5/16 inches taller than the 1938 cab.

Designers stretched the wheelbase again in 1941, this time to 115 inches. This added length translated into more room inside the cab—more legroom, that is, as that 1-1/2-inch gain was found between the cowl and the dash face. This extra space at the driver's feet allowed the seat

back to be reclined to a more comfortable angle; that seat also adjusted to four different positions. New at the driver's right foot was a more convenient, conventional gas pedal in place of the dexterity-testing "button" found on the floorboards of earlier pickups.

That new-for-1941 foot-feed shot the juice to a higher-compression (6.5:1) six-cylinder now rated at 90 horsepower. Those extra horses might have made all the headlines that year if not for another upgrade found beneath the hood. Mounted to the left of the Stovebolt six was a Saginaw recirculating-ball steering box in place of the antiquated worm-and-sector gear used previously. Reportedly, this new equipment reduced steering effort by half—a major step toward the kinder, gentler, much-easier-to-handle pickups of today.

Increased convenience and comfort represent two key advancements in the American pickup's modernization. But equally important has been the extra attention given to style, flair, and class over the years. One of the earliest big styling steps for Chevy trucks also came in 1941. Who can forget that art-deco waterfall grille complemented by those trendy headlights faired into the fenders? This radically reformed look mimicked impressions first made by Chevrolet's automobile line in 1940, yet it still possessed a distinctive persona all its own. And distinctive was crucial, as reflected by all that Ford started doing in 1938 to increase the pizzazz of its pickups.

As it had been before and always will be, competitive forces were also key to American pickup progress before World War II. The battle between Ford and Chevrolet during the 1930s and 1940s grew more intense every year, with customers benefiting most from the ground gained. The harder the two rivals fought, the better their pickups got. And the best was still yet to come.

First In Peace

The Advance-Design Years:

1947–1955

Above
Chevrolet's first Advance-Design pickup appeared in the summer of 1947. New features included a roomier cab with larger doors for easier entry and exit. Also notice the hidden door hinges, a design touch that would soon be the trend throughout the truck field.

Left
Chevrolet trucks were top sellers again after World War II thanks to the introduction of the all-new Advance-Design models. The last Advance-Design trucks were built in early 1955. The gorgeous Medium Cream Chevy half-ton shown here is a 1954 model.

Chevrolet barely had a chance to show off its radically restyled "art-deco" trucks before America was forced into a worldwide war for the second time. Wartime rationing and restrictions were enacted within a few weeks after the Pearl Harbor attack of December 7, 1941, and among the many things Americans soon found themselves doing without were new vehicles. Chevrolet's last pre-war pickup left the line, wonderfully wacky waterfall grille and all, at the end of January 1942.

Things certainly looked bleak then, but the tide of battle quickly turned, and Washington began to relax its hold on Detroit ever so slightly in 1944. By the time Operation Overlord swamped the beaches of Normandy on June 6, at least some new trucks had been released to the public, these going to high-priority civilian customers in the business of keeping this country up and running. Chevrolet had been allowed to begin building trucks for certain farmers, factory owners, and the like in January.

"Chevrolet's popular pick-up truck is in production again, because the Government recognized the importance of this versatile vehicle to agriculture, industry and trade," explained a magazine ad early in 1945. "Of course, production is limited—still, thousands of essential users will be enabled to procure these high-utility units. Better see your Chevrolet dealer now, if your business makes you eligible to purchase a new truck."

Chevrolet actually started selling trucks to civilians before World War II ended, as part of a plan to keep vital American businesses solvent.

Come spring 1945, America was running on all eight cylinders and Allied military forces were poised for the final assault on their Axis enemies. Germany succumbed in May, Japan in August. Detroit roared back to life immediately thereafter.

Americans were soon buying Chevy trucks again. On the other hand, Chevrolet's first postwar passenger cars didn't start showing up at dealerships until November. That new pickups appeared before new automobiles in 1945 was no surprise, considering the head start given to limited truck manufacturing by the War Production Board more than a year before peace came. "Hence, when the war was won, it was not necessary to reconvert lines, and continued production averted an acute truck shortage," wrote Chevrolet chief engineer John Woods in 1947.

Chevrolet built the last of its preferred-customer pickups (mostly identified as 1944 and 1945 models) on August 31, 1945. Regular production of "new" 1946 models commenced the next day—new because these CK-model trucks looked an awful lot like those 1944-1945 renditions, which in turn were plainly reminiscent of their 1942 forerunners right down to their BK-model designations. Chevrolet officials themselves even hesitated to tout the arrival of an honest-to-goodness, truly new peacetime pickup after the CK half-ton hit the streets. According to service bulletins, "these [trucks] are not to be considered postwar models [as] they do represent a continuation of the regular 1942 lines."

For that reason historians today refer to the CK as an "interim" model. The last of these was built on September 1, 1946. Some early CK pickups were actually

titled as 1945 models, while some later BKs were registered as '46s. As confusing as this may sound, a "second-series" 1946 truck, the DP, went into production on May 1, 1946, to cloud matters even further.

While the DP also looked very much like those art-deco trucks of 1942, it was considered a new postwar pickup thanks to various not-so-obvious upgrades that helped set it apart from the CK. Glass sealing was improved throughout the DP cab as was weather-stripping. More durable seat covers were included, and the rear bumper and fenders were reinforced. Both bumpers, as well as the grille, hubcaps, door handles, and windshield center post, were chromed instead of painted like comparable CK components. Optional leather upholstery—last seen, like all that gleaming brightwork, in 1942—returned for the DP half-ton, too.

This time, promotional people were more than willing to boldly announce a next generation's arrival. Their proclamation began:

"To help refill the war-depleted highways of America as soon as possible, Chevrolet presents, with no engineering delay, new lines of time-tested trucks for 1946. Based on the 1941 model vehicles, our last truly prewar trucks and the best-designed trucks Chevrolet has ever manufactured heretofore, the new trucks are improved by the experience gained in five years of developing military trucks, five years of intense research in materials, five years of study of the operation of Chevrolet trucks on the largest proving ground in the world ... the highways of America ... in the particularly tough job of war transportation."

And the advertising people didn't need to proclaim it twice.

Pre-war leftover or not, Chevrolet's DP pickup brought buyers running like there was no yesterday —like they had no memories. No one seemed to care that they were taking delivery of old news. If ever a sellers' market—a yanking-candy-from-a-baby's-grasp seller's market—existed in Detroit, it was in 1946. Anything would' have looked brand spanking new to horsepower-hungry Americans that year, and the fully familiar 1946 Chevy was rolling proof. DP trucks picked up right where their AK ancestors had left off in 1941—in first place by a wide margin atop

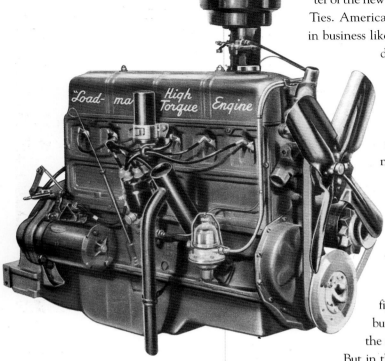

Advance-Design trucks were segregated into the Thriftmaster (light- and medium-duty) and Loadmaster (heavy-duty) models. All of the Thriftmasters and the lightest Loadmaster trucks used the 90-horsepower 216-ci Thriftmaster six-cylinder, while Chevy's heaviest trucks used this Loadmaster six, a 93-horse 235-cube engine.

industry rankings. Slightly more than a quarter of the new trucks built in 1946 wore Bow Ties. America's best-selling truck was back in business like that business had never shut down, and 1946 was just the beginning.

Most curbside kibitzers around Detroit that year probably recognized that such a supreme sellers' market couldn't last for long. Somebody simply had to step up with something certifiably new. Then competitive juices would surely start boiling over, shove would follow push, and before anyone knew it the sellers would be the ones fighting amongst each other for buyers' attentions. Such would be the case soon enough in the 1950s. But in the late-1940s it was still buyers doing all the pushing and shoving.

In the automotive realm it was left to the independents, not the Big Three, to get market waters bubbling. South Bend's Studebaker became, according to its brochures, "the first by far with a postwar car" in 1947. Fresh-faced fellow independent Kaiser-Frazer also made its big splash that year, and two other outsiders, Hudson and Packard, launched their own modernized models in 1948. GM finally jumped in too with its all-new 1948 Cadillac. Chrysler and Ford followed suit in 1949, as did Chevrolet.

The roles were reversed on the truck side as the Big Three got the jump on their independent rivals. Both Ford and Dodge introduced their first postwar commercial vehicles in 1948, but they still couldn't best the industry's entrenched leader. This country's first clearly new peacetime pickup had debuted the year before courtesy of the company that had then been doing it better than any other for 10 straight years.

As they had done in 1936, Chevy truck marketeers began 1947 with the previous year's model continuing basically unchanged. DP production simply rolled over from 1946 before ending its run on May 31, 1947.

Production of second-series 1947 trucks began about a week later, and all comparisons with 1936 quickly faded from there. Announced to the public on June 28, 1947, Chevrolet's new postwar pickup was much more than just a dressed-up variation on an existing theme. Perhaps its name said it all: "Advance-Design."

This time truck buyers knew full well that they were looking at the future, not living in the past. Overall impressions were newer than new, thanks first and foremost to Chevrolet's sensational "Load Proportioned" restyle that owed nothing to car-line trends or pre-war fads. Modernized lines were more pleasing as fender tops, hoodline, and cab roof seemed to work together aesthetically far more cooperatively than ever before. Gone were those old-fashioned pods previously perched atop each front fender. Advance-Design headlights were now fitted nicely within those fenders. Door hinges too were concealed within the body to help further enhance those smooth, clean lines.

Those new impressions were reflected across both new model lines. Light- and medium-duty (half- to one-ton) Advance-Design trucks were Thriftmasters; everything heavier (one-and-one-half- to two-ton) fell into the Loadmaster category. Family ties were obvious, even on the flat-faced cab-over-engine (COE) two-ton. Other conventional Loadmasters used longer fenders and hoods compared to their lighter little brothers. But all models regardless of size (including the snub-nosed COE) relied on the same Thriftmaster cab. And all hoods were alligator jaw units; instead of swinging up to each side in two pieces, the one-piece, rear-hinged Advance-Design lid yawned wide open from the front like a gator's snout, a convenience pioneered in the pickup field by Ford before World War II.

Discounting the passenger compartment, improvements beneath the Advance-Design skin in 1947 were minimal, as the old, reliable Stovebolt continued on in yeoman fashion. The Thriftmaster six was a 90-horsepower 216-ci engine, while the hard-working Loadmaster six displaced 235 cubic inches and produced 93 horses. Lighter Loadmaster trucks used the smaller Thriftmaster six-cylinder, but the bigger haulers all demanded the bigger engine. In light-duty Thriftmaster ranks, a beefed-up frame and mildly upgraded steering gear represented the bulk of the big news from an engineering perspective. That was not to say, however, that Chevy's Advance-Design trucks relied on fresh looks alone to turn heads.

The product of a truly advanced design process, that new cab was as attractive inside as outside, thanks to a long list (30) of trend-setting features that, according to brochures, added up to "Chevrolet's greatest contribution to driver comfort, convenience and safety." This contribution came about after designers had finally gone directly to truck drivers to get their seat-of-the-pants responses. Some historians like to credit Ford for popularizing the ergonomic study procedure in the truck field—most prominently when Dearborn designers

Above
Additions to the 1949 Advance-Design truck included model-series badges for the hood; again, "3100" signified a half-ton. Another 1949 modification involved relocating the gas tank back inside the cab behind the seat.

Left
Though you'd probably never guess it, this 1950 cab-over-engine (COE) Chevrolet Loadmaster truck used the same cab as its smaller Thriftmaster pickup. Fenders and that snub-nosed hood, of course, did not interchange.

Chevy in World War II *Building to Win the War*

Isolationist beliefs ran strong in this country during the 1930s, just as they had 20 years before while the Great War raged "over there," but it was only a matter of time before the United States would be involved in another war. Much of this planet was wracked by military conflict and we Americans were still living our daily lives safe and sound. It wasn't our soil being threatened. It wasn't our citizens dying. Why should we get involved?

By the end of 1940, German forces had stepped into Paris and were threatening Churchill's island fortress. Franklin Roosevelt had sent England's Navy destroyers left over from the last war, but that was about it. Even as late as the fall of 1941 the U.S. was still keeping its hands clean. We watched as London burned and the Far East bled as bright red as the Rising Sun flag encroached upon it.

Then came December 7, 1941. It took the deaths of more than 2,200 U.S. sailors and airmen at Pearl Harbor to finally awaken this sleeping giant. World peace became Washington's business within hours of Japan's surprise attack in the Pacific, and soon Johnny marched off to fight in what was truly a world war.

Meanwhile, America's industrial machinery shifted gears to meet the military's demands for the tools of war. Plow shares were being hammered into swords at a rate never seen before in human history—and fortunately it hasn't been seen since.

Detroit became the greatest contributor to this unprecedented explosion of manufacturing might. Peacetime production of cars and light-trucks was traded for incredibly efficient assembly lines that spit out everything from aircraft engines to complete four-engined bombers. By 1943 America's automakers were building guns, tanks, planes, and ships in numbers that soon had Hirohito and Hitler wishing they had never helped put those cogs in motion.

Chevrolet began its conversion from civilian operation to military mass-production early in 1942. The last Chevy automobile built for public sale rolled off the assembly line on January 30, 1942. Every plant except one went to work winning the war with the division's "Volume for Victory" banner waving high overhead. The lone automobile facility, the Saginaw Service Manufacturing Plant, remained as it was to supply service parts for the millions of Chevrolet cars and trucks that would have to hang in there until war's end. In all, the company devoted 16 million square feet of floor space to the war effort before Washington finally

Chevrolet plants produced everything from guns to shells to airplane engines during World War II. Trucks, too, were built by the boatload.

authorized the resumption of civilian automobile production in the summer of 1945.

Chevrolet's first new postwar cars—1942 models with 1946 designations—rolled off the line in October 1945. After the Office of Defense Transportation suspended the ration of new commercial vehicles, civilian truck production geared back up as well with basically the same vehicles from 1942. As early as January 1944, Chevrolet had been allowed to build trucks for select civilian customers working in fields critical to the war effort. While some half-tons were released through these channels, most trucks that made it onto farms and into fire departments were one-and-one-half-ton machines.

Additional pickups were built by Chevrolet between 1942 and 1945, but these went right into military service. The division also supplied a long olive-drab line of heavy-duty haulers to U.S. fighting forces, including everything from ambulances and six-wheel-drive trucks, to armored cars. Chevrolet manufactured nearly a half-million military vehicles during the war, and that wasn't all.

The company also manufactured millions of high-explosive and armor-piercing shells, thousands of 90mm anti-aircraft guns, and millions of pounds of forgings (aluminum and steel) and castings (iron and magnesium) for other military projects. Chevrolet's advertising execs were especially proud of all the aircraft engines assembled under license from Pratt & Whitney. As of November 1944, Chevrolet had built about 54,000 P&W radial powerplants, including a 1,200-horsepower 14-cylinder version for the B-24 Liberator bomber (manufactured at break-neck speeds by Ford, incidentally), a similar 14-cylinder engine for C-47 and C-53 transport planes, and a 2,000-horsepower, 18-cylinder monster for the P-61 Black Widow night fighter and P-47 Thunderbolt.

By November 1943, Chevrolet was assembling 3,500 combat aircraft engines a month, which, in the words of those beaming admen, was "the largest single month's production ever achieved by any aircraft engine manufacturer up to and including that date." According to the same 1945 ad, Chevrolet's "ever-increasing production of war materiel has dwarfed all previous production records of even America's largest manufacturers of motor cars and trucks."

When peace arrived in 1945, Chevrolet picked up right where it had left off before the war and proceeded to lead Ford into an age of new prosperity. Soon no production record in the truck field would be safe.

created their original F-100. But once again Chevrolet was first.

Chevy pollsters had gone to work right after the war. Their nationwide survey showed most Americans agreed about one major complaint: despite various upgrades made to pre-war pickups, postwar truck cabs were still cramped and uncomfortable. Safety too remained an issue, as most respondents complained further of limited outward visibility.

Bingo! Buyers spoke and Chevrolet listened. The Advance-Design interior welcomed customers with real roominess and newfound convenience. Driver confidence was enhanced too by the fully welded, all-steel cab strengthened by its Unisteel Battleship construction. Door openings were widened four inches to make entrance and exit a breeze, and total standard window size was up 15 percent. If that wasn't enough visibility for you, there was also the "Nu-Vue" option that added two more pieces of safety glass to the passenger compartment's rear corners. The resulting five-window cab sported a 40 percent increase in glass area to give drivers "Observation Car Vision."

Increased roominess was the result of a wider, longer cab. The former dimension went up eight inches, the latter seven. Those widened parameters translated into eight more inches of hip room and 3.5 inches of extra shoulder space, while the added length made for another foot for the feet.

Another comfort and convenience enhancement resulted from an inclined adjustable seat that raised upward as it moved forward to keep the driver's head at an optimum viewing level. And more springs in that seat meant less fatigue in your seat, as well as those of two fellow riders. That's right, the Advance-Design truck's wider seat could fit three adults side-by-side in reasonable comfort—as long as those guys all knew each other reasonably well. Just try stuffing a trio of fully-grown (or partially for that matter) men inside a pre-war pickup. After 1947, real three-passenger seating became one of the bigger bragging points made when rival pickups were introduced.

As mentioned, both Ford and Dodge responded with modernized trucks of their own in 1948. Studebaker's beautifully restyled postwar pickup debuted for 1949, then stuck around in the same basic form for 10 more

years as the cash-strapped independent couldn't afford anything more than minor updates. Far more financially sound than its Indiana rival, Chicago-based International Harvester introduced its new L-series pickup as a 1950 model and followed it with upgraded R- and S-series replacements in 1953 and 1956, respectively. Dodge also freshened the face of its B-series "Pilot House" truck in 1951 and 1953 before rolling out a new C-series in 1954. Meanwhile, Ford stayed with its Bonus-Built F-series pickups until the fabled F-100 debuted in 1953 to help take the truck market up to its next level.

None of these competitive actions seemed to matter much to Chevrolet, however. Apparently its new-for-1947 truck design was so advanced it didn't require any major upgrades for eight years. The same basic package rolled on into 1955 with no complaints from customers who continued to make Chevrolet

Vent windows appeared in the doors of Advance-Design pickups in 1951. This 1951 Chevy is a 3800-series one-ton with a nine-foot-long bed.

Model-series badges returned to Chevy pickup hoods in 1953 after Korean War supply restrictions had limited the use of such frivolous chrome in 1951. This 1953 half-ton is also fitted with optional trim rings on each wheel.

number one year in, year out. Ford still couldn't catch up, not even with its new F-1 in 1948.

Chevrolet truck sales jumped up every year from 1946 to 1950 and probably would have again in 1951 had not wartime restrictions once more emerged to put a lid on things. Nineteen-forty-seven's sales were 29 percent higher than 1946's, and 1948's went up another 25 percent. The increase was only 8 percent for 1949, but a downturn at Ford led to one of the widest victory

margins ever for Chevrolet: the longtime leader built roughly 70 percent more trucks than its closest rival that year. Although Ford rebounded big-time in 1950, it again didn't matter, as Chevrolet celebrated the arrival of a new decade with a record performance that wasn't topped until 1963.

Calendar-year production had breached the 300,000-unit level for only the second time (the first came in 1941) in 1947 on the way to a new all-time

high. Chevy's market share that year had been 27 percent. In 1950 the division roared past the 400,000 plateau and almost reached the half-million mark. Nearly 46,000 trucks were built in August alone, a new record by far. Nineteen-fifty's market share may not have been a record, but at 36.8 percent (again measured by calendar-year production) it represented one of the heftiest hunks of the truck pie ever carved out.

Government regulations then took over late in 1950 as the Korean Conflict flared up. But while sales fell 16 percent in 1951, Chevrolet still continued to lead Ford by many lengths and did so again in 1952 after another big drop. Federal restrictions were finally lifted in February 1953 just in time to help Dearborn close the gap considerably with its fashionably fresh F-100. Yet there was the challenger showing off its second new postwar pickup in five years, and the reigning champ was still leading the way comfortably with the same truck it had introduced in 1947. If it ain't broke, don't fix it. Indeed. By December 31, 1953, Chevrolet officials could count more than 3 million trucks they'd built since the end of

Left
The snazziest pickups offered during the Advance-Design years had the five-window cab. Called the "Nu-Vue" option by Chevrolet, this cab featured two extra windows at each rear corner of the cab.

Below
The Chevy pickup cab was about as classy, comfortable, and convenient as it got in the light-truck ranks in 1953.

The standard 3100-series power source in 1953 was still the 216.5-ci Thriftmaster six-cylinder, rated at 92 horsepower.

65

Above
Options and accessories grew more plentiful during the 1950s.

Far right
As in 1947, Chevrolet's 1955 truck line began the model year with a carryover from the previous year, meaning both first- and second-series pickups were again offered. This 1955 first-series Chevy is decked out with loads of options, including extra chrome, full wheel covers, and that big, bright hood "bird."

World War II, meaning the division was far from broke.

Though the Advance-Design trucks apparently needed no fixing prior to 1954, they were treated to a decent dose of typical updates, some important, many not so. Included in the latter group were various styling tweaks, beginning in 1949 with the addition of bright emblems to the hood-sides that now denoted load capacity: "3100" for the half-ton, "3600" for the three-quarter-ton, and "3800" for the one-ton. Also new that year was a revised paint scheme for the basic grille—as it had been in 1947 and 1948, chrome plating was an option up front in 1949. Standard grilles in 1947 and 1948 had been painted completely in the same shade as the body. Nineteen-forty-nine's grille bars were accented with silver-gray paint in their recesses, an addition that helped emphasize the unit's depth and width.

Appearances at the opposite end changed on many 1951 Chevy trucks as part of a re-emphasis on convenience. Some customers had complained earlier about tailgate operation: the gate could only drop down a bit past 45 degrees because the bumper stopped it there. No problem. The previously standard rear bumper was moved to the options list in 1951. With no bumper in the way, the tailgate could be lowered all the way into a straight-down position, an occasionally required convenience familiar to most pickup owners. And to minimize potential damage in back to a bumperless truck, the taillight, tailpipe, license plate bracket, and spare tire carrier were all redone to allow at least some collision protection from the cargo box.

Another change involving bumpers began surfacing midway through 1951. Wartime shortages forced Chevrolet to delete unnecessary brightwork, meaning that

bumpers and hubcaps were all painted instead of chromed by 1952. The optional chrome grille was temporarily shelved too, as were the bright model-series badges that had been added to the hood three years before.

Series-number badges (restyled but still on the hood) returned in 1953, along with chromed hubcaps and optional chrome for the grille and add-on rear bumper. New attractive options that year included tinted glass and a side-mounted spare tire for the cargo box just behind the driver's door.

Additional expansion included an even wider seat for 1950 pickups, to make seating a trio across even easier. Designers had previously re-addressed this issue in 1949 when they removed the parking brake and gearshift levers from their traditional spot on the floor to spare a middle-seated male passenger any unwanted injury, pain, and/or embarrassment. The three-speed shifter was relocated to the steering column, and a parking brake pedal was added to the driver's left.

More convenient (and trendy) vent windows appeared on the doors in 1951 and instantly eliminated the need for the driver's side cowl vent found on 1947–1950 Advance-Design trucks. Equally trendy (and more convenient) pushbutton exterior door-latch releases replaced simple door handles in 1952. A lockable driver's door option also debuted that year; previous trucks only featured a key-lock for the passenger-side door.

Although engineering upgrades were few, they were important. First came a new, optional four-speed transmission in 1948, with less-gnarly, easier-to-shift synchromesh gears. Chevrolet was the first to offer a synchronized four-speed to truck buyers, yet adding one to an Advance-Design pickup required the return of that middleman-threatening floor shifter. Engineers also made various improvements to both six-cylinders, Thriftmaster and Loadmaster, in 1948 to increase durability and simplicity. Included were better bearings, a stronger crankshaft, and lighter synthetic-rubber valve seals. In 1950 the Thriftmaster six was uprated to 92 horsepower to better reflect the upgrades made since its pre-war days.

Also in 1950 the antiquated knee-action shock absorbers used on earlier 3100-series pickups were replaced by double-acting aircraft-style shocks. Light-duty trucks received better brakes as well in 1951. These new self-energizing stoppers provided more braking power with less

A Semi Conversion *Semi Tough*

This unique 1947 first-series Chevy truck's dual-wheels were apparently added some 50 years ago as part of a dealer promotion. The fifth-wheel and trailer were supplied as a conversion kit by the Mustang Texas Sheet Metal and Manufacturing Company, of Dallas.

Chevrolet's truck line has always featured its fair share of diversity. From compact pickups to open-road big-rigs, GM's low-priced leader has built it. Chevrolet didn't exactly make a half-ton tractor-trailer, but contributed to the construction of one.

When Chevy enthusiast Steve Tate, of Liberty, Missouri, found this oddball in 1999, he knew he'd stumbled upon something unique. This former Chevrolet dealer claims he really wasn't interested in adding another vintage vehicle to his corral. Nonetheless, when Steve heard about a strange pickup converted into a "mini-semi," he couldn't resist. A 90-mile trek ensued to Malta Bend, Missouri, where he met A. J. McRoberts IV.

"Upon arriving at the homestead, we went directly to the old blacksmiths shop and began digging the doors open," recalled Tate in 2001. "My eyes couldn't believe what they were seeing: there sat a 1947 first-series truck and trailer still parked in the same spot where it had been for 26 years. This truck had a fifth-wheel mounted in back and 6.00x16 dual rear wheels, which were still holding air. Setting beside it was a 12-foot, factory-made, combination grain/livestock trailer. The aluminum trailer had a wood floor, removable wood sides, and an aluminum rounded bulkhead."

Tate took the truck home the following weekend. With the help of Eldon Taylor, of Taylor Chevrolet in Maysville, Missouri, he had "Little Feller" up in running with next to no sweat. "Eldon replaced the points, plugs, fuel pump, soaked the carburetor, cleaned the starter, and changed the oil," Steve added. "She started right off and purred like a kitten."

According to A. J. McRoberts IV, his father had attended a county fair in 1947 and discovered this concoction on display by Chevrolet Motor Division's Kansas City zone office. McRoberts III went to his local dealer, Mason Chevrolet in Lexington, Missouri, and asked about buying a similar tractor-trailer setup.

"Mason Chevrolet contacted the Chevrolet zone office and was told the unit A. J. [McRoberts III] had seen was going to be up for sale after the display was finished," continued Tate. "Apparently Chevrolet had contracted Mustang Trailer, or their local distributor, to build this unit as a unique special promotion. I spoke with Harold Melton with Melton Chevrolet in Belleville, Kansas. Melton is a Chevrolet dealer that has specialized in trucks since 1944. Harold remembers similar promotions run through the Wichita zone office."

Tate also has some additional supportive evidence: a copy of a sales brochure from the Mustang Texas Sheet Metal and Manufacturing Company, of Dallas, Texas. Fifty-some years back, this firm marketed a fifth-wheel trailer conversion for half-, three-quarter- and one-ton trucks of any make—the brochure depicts a typical installation on the company's own 1947 Ford half-ton.

"A pick-up owner may have occasional 'medium-weight' loads to haul, but not often enough to justify the additional investment in a larger truck," began this brochure. "For those heavier jobs, snap a Mustang Trailer on your pick-up and you are ready to go. This husky unit meets the long recognized need for a light, conventional type trailer that can be handled by a pick-up."

Aluminum had become the hot ticket during the years immediately following World War II. Siding, mobile homes, boats—if it needed to be lighter and stronger, this trendy metal was the way to go. This was a fact not lost on countless enterprising entrepreneurs, including one particular outfit in Texas. "Aluminum construction provides 60 percent less weight and 20 percent greater yield strength than most materials used in trailer construction," added the Mustang Trailers brochure.

Specifications listed a 1.5-ton capacity for the seven-foot wide trailer that rolled on dual "truck-type" wheels shod in 6.50x16 six-ply tires. Braking was by a Wagner Electric vacuum-controlled hydraulic system (with quick disconnect coupling) with an easily mounted steering column activation unit. Two trailer lengths were available: 15 feet was standard, and 12 was optional. Weight was about 1,660 pounds for the 12-foot option, and 1,840 for the 15. Buyers could select slatted or solid removable sides to haul grain or livestock, and the aluminum nose section lifted off for an easy conversion into an unlimited flatbed.

The complete conversion itself was just as quick and easy, at least according to the brochure: "Only 7 minutes to snap on a Mustang." The fifth-wheel was held in place by four bolts and was "a one man job" to install, and the pickup box could be removed by himself as well. According to the instructions, "an 'A' frame, the beam in your garage, or a limb of a tree will serve just as well" as a suspension point for the box's removal. Once the fifth-wheel was bolted in place, it was time to back up and hitch up the trailer.

The transformation of a light-truck into a semi was just that simple, as was returning it to its original form. "Let the bed of the pick-up hang there," instructed the company paperwork. "When finished with the hauling job, lower the Mustang landing gear and drive the pick-up out. Remove the fifth wheel. Back the pick-up under the truck bed. Lower the bed on the chassis and bolt on."

The truck's dual rear wheels were undoubtedly added as part of the original promotional ploy. Whether the installation occurred at a dealership or the assembly plant is unknown. Although it was a wise modification, the added strength apparently wasn't necessarily required: the Mustang brochure shows a standard pickup rear axle in its application.

Tate's Mustang trailer application today awaits restoration, a job that wouldn't be all that much tougher, relatively speaking, than the original conversion. He doesn't think he'll tackle the project, but he'd love to see someone step up and give Little Feller a good home. Any takers?

pedal pressure and were easier to service. The system also featured longer lining life and improved sealing to resist higher levels of invasive dust, dirt and moisture.

So by 1954 Chevrolet's Advance-Design pickups could stop with the best of them. They were as colorful as any other half-tons on the market, and they still held their own in the comfort and convenience categories, —almost. Ford had beaten Chevy to the punch with a kinder, gentler automatic-transmission pickup in 1953. On top of that, the F-100 was then fitted optionally with Dearborn's first overhead-valve V-8 the following year. Nonetheless Chevrolet continued leading in sales despite the painful fact that it was the only member of the Big Three left without a modern V-8. Chevy was also the lone ranger in the shiftless driving department—Dodge trucks first real automatic was still two years away, but at least it did have its semi-automatic option in 1953.

While Chevy's sales did slip in 1954, the lead over Ford remained significant. And distant Dodge was in the early stages of a downhill slide that would continue into the 1960s. International was never a threat, Willys-Overland had its own off-road game all to itself, and Studebaker was dead and didn't know it. Chevrolet's own history-making response to Ford's F-100 was then waiting in the wings, leaving GM's dominating truck division in an enviable position: at the top with little to worry about and nothing to do but have a little fun with the final Advance-Design rendition. This time the best was saved for last.

More major changes were made for 1954 than in all the other years combined since 1947. A new one-piece curved windshield debuted, as did a new grille (that was especially dazzling when chromed), new parking lights, a new instrument panel, new interior colors and trim, and a new steering wheel. New as well was a deeper cargo box that, working in concert with a reshaped rear frame section, lowered the half-ton's loading height by two inches. The 1954 frame was also fitted with a heavier cross-member at the rear of the engine to improve rigidity. As for that improved pickup box, it worked so well it remained in place nearly unchanged until 1988.

All that aside, the really big news involved a nice collection of new and improved powertrain parts. First and foremost was 1954's base engine, the Thriftmaster 235.

Formerly limited to the largest Loadmaster trucks, the bigger, better 235-ci Stovebolt six became the standard power source for all Chevrolet trucks in 1954, as the 216 was finally dropped. The Thriftmaster 235 featured full-pressure lubrication (a Chevy pickup first), higher 7.5:1 compression, aluminum pistons, beefier connecting rods, and a stronger crankshaft. Connecting rod bearings were now modern insert-types. Output for both the Thriftmaster 235 and its Loadmaster 235 twin was 112 horsepower.

A new, heavier 10-inch clutch also became standard for the 1954 3100-series pickup to better handle those extra horses. Two optional transmissions were introduced too: a heavy-duty synchromesh three-speed and the four-speed Hydra-Matic, Chevrolet's first truck-line automatic.

Additional extra-cost features abounded in 1954, as the options list nearly doubled in size compared to 1953's. Among the more intriguing were car-style full-width wheel covers, an eye-catching big-bird hood ornament, two-tone paint, and Deluxe cab treatments. That latter option was making a return appearance following a brief hiatus mandated by Korean War restrictions. Included in this deal were rear corner windows, bright-metal trim for the door glass, dual horns, a visor and armrest for the passenger, a cigar lighter, and two-tone interior appointments. Chrome treatment for the bumpers, grille, and hubcaps was not included as part of the Deluxe cab package but could be ordered separately.

If things had gone as planned, 1954 would have been the final year for the Advance-Design line. A new era awaited GM's low-priced division in 1955, but only for the car side initially. Chevrolet's all-new automobiles took priority, leaving the company's truck makers briefly to play second fiddle while all attentions focused on the Hot One. All-new trucks being readied for a 1955 introduction had to wait for their day in the sun.

This meant that the 1954 pickup had to carry over into the 1955 model year, creating yet another first-series/second-series situation. Though some trim did change from 1954 to 1955, the only real upgrade was a switch from the closed torque-tube drive to a modern Hotchkiss-type open driveshaft. All other features remained the same. Again, this was not a problem. Chevy trucks were still number one, and the word on the street was that the next generation was on its way. It arrived in March 1955.

Left
All 1955 Chevy pickups used the same cargo box first introduced in 1954. And all Chevrolet trucks from 1955 to 1987 (Stepsides, that is) continued using the same basic structure.

Below
Optional full wheel covers began coming into vogue in 1955. Adding the wide-whitewall tires that year was undoubtedly rarely done.

Thoroughly Modern

Task-Force Trucks,
1955–1959

Above
You can't miss those "W-shaped" valve covers. Yes, the famed 409 V-8's forerunner, the 348, did begin life in the late1950s as a truck engine, but for Chevrolet's heavy-duty lines only. The 409 then appeared in 1961 for high-performance passenger-car applications only.

Left
As in 1936 and 1947, Chevrolet began the 1955 model year with a "leftover" first-series model (left) then introduced a brand new second-series truck midyear.

Before 1955, Chevrolet automobiles were best known for being reliable and practical. They were also plentiful, partly due to their reliable, practical nature, but mostly because they were also affordable—make that cheap. Like Ford, Chevrolet always sold so many cars every year because those vehicles were easily within the reach of the masses. "Low-priced" and "leader" didn't go so well together by accident.

That's not to say, however, that Chevrolet was number one for so many years simply because it cut corners better than Ford, Plymouth, and the rest. Although cost-consciousness was key from the beginning, GM product-planners still did their darnedest to put their low-priced division a notch or two above Ford. More car for the money was Chevrolet's main claim to fame dating back to the introduction of a "six in the price range of four" in 1929. Sure, Henry Ford did one-up (or two-up?) his closest challenger with his "eight for the price of four" three years later. But Chevy's overhead-valve Stovebolt still held its own up against Henry's flathead for nearly a quarter-century. Apparently those two extra cylinders mattered little in the minds of buyers, especially so on the truck side of the market.

Those two additional bores began to matter more within the cranial cavities of GM execs after Ford introduced its relatively modern OHV V-8 for both its cars and trucks in 1954. While six-cylinders would remain the meat-and-potatoes motivators among all truck makers throughout the 1950s, the day had finally come for Chevrolet's movers-and-shakers to consider one-upping themselves with a new, modernized power source or risk finally slipping back to number two.

Far right
Ford first tried upstaging Chevrolet Advance-Design trucks with its first F-series pickup in 1948 (left). Ford's historic F-100 then debuted in 1953. Chevy's truck team finally retaliated in 1955 with this beautiful Task Force truck.

Far right insert
The 1955 Chevy pickup's big Panoramic windshield also could have been complemented with optional Panoramic rear glass to maximize both style and visibility. The sidemount spare tire was an option introduced in 1953.

Below
The resemblances up front between Chevrolet's fantastic new Bel Air for 1955 and its equally new pickup were no coincidence. Truck designers that year recognized that style sells.

A modernized pickup was also in order, considering that the aging Advance-Design models were surely wearing out their welcome. They may have fended off Ford's F-1 challenge in 1948, but the all-new F-100 that followed five years later was more than a match for the truck Chevrolet had been marketing in almost unchanged fashion since 1947. By 1953 it was plainly clear to Chevrolet General Manager Thomas Keating that just a facelift, like the one then being readied for the 1954 Chevy truck, wouldn't stand up for long in a morphing marketplace that was changing more rapidly every year. Chief Engineer Ed Cole agreed, as did Sales Manager William Fish.

Typically a man with his finger on the pulse, Fish was especially fond of flashy 1950s fads. Forget more car for the money; "style sells" was his main motto, as it had been around Cadillac, Buick, and Oldsmobile offices since the beginning of the decade. Reliable practicality had served Chevrolet well during the 1930s and 1940s. However, the fast-paced, fashion-conscious 1950s represented an entirely new ballgame, and sales gurus like Fish needed only to look down to Plymouth for proof that postwar fortunes could no longer rely on pre-war perceptions.

Chrysler's low-priced division had surprisingly managed to hang on to its traditional third-place sales ranking from 1946 to '1953—surprisingly because Plymouths were as boring and dull-looking as it got in the early-1950s automotive arena. Function dominated form, as pure practicality remained Plymouth's main selling point, just as it had been before World War II. Crusty conservative thinking then caught up with the veteran firm in a big way in 1954, as production fell off by 40 percent resulting in a plunge to fifth. A revitalized Plymouth wouldn't find third again until 1957. Was it any wonder that Chevrolet cars and trucks were both redesigned in 1955 with an eye towards radically enhancing style and flair?

On the car side, Claire MacKichan's creative staff handled style, while Cole's engineers addressed flair. Results in each case were historic. MacKichan's "Futuramic" restyle on its own made the all-new 1955 Chevy an even bigger seller. Never before had affordability looked so good. But when Cole's new optional V-8 was thrown in too as part of the deal, a real legend was born. Chevrolet called it the "Hot One," and for good reason. These babies jumped out of dealers' hands like oven-fresh potatoes, then proceeded to warm drivers' blood quicker than cars costing half again as much, or more. Detroit's bottom shelf no longer would be such a bland place to shop for everyday transportation.

The heart of the Hot One did not represent Chevrolet's first venture into V-8 production, as is often reported. Chevy's original V-8 had actually appeared in 1917, then quickly disappeared the next year. That said, the vaunted small-block of 1955 does deserve pioneer status basically because its forerunner was a flop and it wasn't. A true milestone is actually a fair description. When Ford made huge headlines in 1932 with America's first eight-for-the-great-unwashed, it did so with a small, clunky, L-head V-8 that constituted nearly as much old news as new. For the most part, power

Above
Car-line style also carried over inside the 1955 Chevy pickup. A new, flashy dash and optional deluxe appointments were the main attractions.

Right
Chevy's new overhead-valve V-8 was called the "Trademaster 265" when found beneath truck hoods. Trademaster output was 145 horsepower.

potential was sharply limited, too. When Chevy engineers unveiled their first modern V-8 23 years later, they looked only to the sky for a limit. Never before had triple digits on the speedometer come so cheaply. Power to the people indeed.

In the works since just before Ed Cole came on board in 1952, Chevrolet's lightweight, compact OHV small-block displaced 265 cubic inches and wound out like no other V-8 ever seen. Its very short three-inch stroke helped make that high rev limit possible, as did its innovative valvetrain layout. Instead of using typical rocker arms hung on a central shaft, the 265 V-8 featured lighter, less complicated stamped-steel rockers, each mounted separately on a ball-pivot stud.

Standard output was 162 horses beneath a 1955 Bel Air hood. In truck trim the new Trademaster 265 was rated at 145 horsepower. When combined with thoroughly modernized sheet metal, Chevy's first V-8 helped transform the company's latest, greatest pickup far and away into the most attractive buy on the market.

The 1955 commercial-line restyle job had been assigned to Luther "Lu" Stier, head of Chevrolet's truck studio from 1949 to 1962. Like MacKichan, Stier had various talented designers to rely on. Among these was Charles Jordan, the same Chuck Jordan who later rose up to become GM's executive design chief. Jordan basically cut his teeth on light-truck design work after initially joining GM as an eager apprentice in the experimental styling studio in 1949. Fortunately for Stier, the experimental studio was located near his lair inside Fisher Body Plant 8. Jordan had always been interested in trucks—his MIT graduate thesis was titled "Heavy-Duty Mack Truck Styling"—so it was only a matter of time before the two hooked up.

Jordan worked briefly under Stier before being called to duty with the Air Force Reserves in 1952. While serving in a military art studio at Florida's Cape Canaveral, 2nd Lt. Jordan began dreaming of an entirely new pickup. When not working on official assignments, he would sketch various truly stylish trucks: sleek, sexy stunners that put most automobile designs of the day to shame. Jordan the civilian brought these sketches along to show his boss after returning to Detroit in 1953. Stier's team at the time was busy drawing up Chevrolet's next truck restyle, so the door was wide open to free thinking.

Many of Jordan's fabulously fresh ideas reached reality in the form of the gorgeous Cameo Carrier, the car-style classic built from 1955 to 1958. But the legendary designer also played a major role in reshaping the standard 1955 Chevy pickup. As Stier told *Special Interest Autos* editor Michael Lamm in 1977, 1955's "basic front-end sheet metal was very much the design of young Chuck Jordan. Bob Phillips also contributed much to this program. The interior layout, gauges, upholstery, and so forth became the responsibility of Drew Hare, who was then chief designer for truck interiors."

Various reflections of MacKichan's work showed up in Stier's studio to demonstrate family ties, once more, from the car side to the truck. But instead of being the product of necessity, as had been the case before World War II, this clear commonality resulted from a precise plan. This time the goal was to allow the 1955 pickup to bask in at least some of the Hot One's limelight, while proving that trucks could look damn near as pretty as their automotive cousins and still be tough. Style definitely did sell cars during the 1950s. And Chevrolet's top brass wanted to prove once and for all that the same tactic could work just as well for trucks. That it did. It was the 1955 Chevy truck's newfound style and flair—punctuated most dramatically by the cool, clean Cameo with its tantalizing fiberglass tail—that helped turn the corner sharper than ever before toward trucks' rampant popularity today.

Featuring sharply sculptured lines contrasted by soft, rounded corners, the 1955 second-series truck showed off its car-line connections primarily up front, where those hooded headlights and sporty "eggcrate" grille clearly mimicked the Futuramic facade. Equally prominent was the familiar one-piece "Panoramic" windshield that wrapped around at the corners just like the trend-setting front glass first shown off on various upscale GM automobiles in 1953.

Curved, one-piece windshields were nothing new on the pickup market in 1955—International had introduced this stylish touch in 1950, and Chevrolet's first had come in 1954. But these gently bent sheets of glass paled in comparison to the rakish wraparound front

Above
Lightweight, compact construction, a short stroke, and individual ball-stud rocker arms were a few of the new 265-ci V-8's highlights in 1955. Standard output in passenger-car form was 162 horsepower.

Left
Studebaker made the first big fashion statement in the postwar market in 1948, courtesy of designer Robert Bourke.

4x4 By Chevy

Off and Running Off the Road

Chevrolet first offered a four-wheel-drive pickup direct from the factory in 1957. This rather rare 1959 short-bed 4x4 almost appears taller than it is long. Back then, bolting on a four-wheel-drive transfer case added some serious ground clearance.

Chevrolet didn't invent four-wheel-drive, but it has built some of the best 4x4s around today. You'd never guess that General Motors has only been in the off-road game for barely 45 years.

Corporate cousin GMC actually beat Chevrolet to the punch with its first factory-built 4x4 in 1956, while Chevy followed in 1957. Ford didn't join the fraternity until 1959, the same year as Studebaker. International-Harvester had quietly entered the four-wheel-drive pickup race in 1953, but the competition hadn't started there.

Dodge's world-famous, one-ton Power Wagon had debuted in March 1946 to prove that four-wheel-drive trucks could survive just as well in civilian life as they had on the battlefields of World War II. Those crude, burly "army truck" Power Wagons rolled on up through 1968. Exports to the far ends of the globe continued until 1978.

Many firms, including Chevrolet and GMC, had built 4x4 (and even 6x6) trucks during the war, but only Dodge and Willys-Overland officials chose to take what they had learned from defense contracts and put those lessons to good use in peacetime. Willys' four-wheel-drive Jeep pickup appeared in 1948 to give Dodge some early competition in a market that would take a few decades to really get rolling. Two more Willys 4x4s, the FC-150 and FC-170, debuted in 1957, the same year Dodge slapped its proven Power Wagon badges onto easier-on-the-eye standard pickup sheet-metal. A more civilized three-quarter-ton Power Wagon also appeared for the first time in 1957.

While both Ford and Chevrolet 4x4 pickups had been around before, they weren't exactly "factory-built." Ford's earliest four-wheel-drive pickups had appeared late in 1936 courtesy of contracted conversions made by the Marmon-Herrington company in Indianapolis. Marmon-Herrington Fords stayed on the market until Ford finally cut out the middleman in Indiana and initiated its own in-house 4x4 production 23 years later.

Chevrolet's 4x4 pre-history involved a similar story. By 1950 the Northwestern Auto Parts Company of Minneapolis offered a comparable 4x4 conversion deal for GMC and Chevrolet trucks. While "NAPCO" four-wheel-drive installations also appeared on Fords, Studebakers, and others, the Minnesota firm made the most hay with General Motors.

In business since 1918, Northwestern Auto Parts had also gained some serious momentum during World War II thanks to the influx of federal defense contract work. The company supplied, engineered, and manufactured specialty parts and assemblies for various big-time contractors during the war, and gained much experience in four-wheel-drive mechanics along the way. Following in Dodge and Willys' tracks, Northwestern then continued to be a sub-contractor for the U.S. military during peacetime. Among its more popular postwar products was the "Powr-Pak" 4x4 conversion, which gained fame in the 1950s. By that time the company name had officially changed to NAPCO Industries.

NAPCO's Powr-Pak conversion was so simple: no major cutting or welding was required and the whole operation wrapped itself up in only three hours. Four holes were drilled in the frame, and a small access area was opened in the floorboard for the dual-speed transfer case shifter were the only real modifications. From there it was all wrench-turning.

Along with a dual-range transfer case (with drives of 1:1 and 1.94:1), the Powr-Pak parts list included a short driveshaft to connect that case to the existing Chevrolet four-speed gearbox and another shortened shaft that ran back to the existing rear axle. NAPCO also supplied the mounting bracket that held the transfer case in place with the four frame holes. The rest of the list consisted of a front driveshaft, a modified Chevrolet rear axle fitted with Bendix-Weiss constant-velocity joints to allow steerable wheels up front, and spacer blocks that fit between the springs and the axles to ensure clearance between the front differential housing and the engine's oil pan.

Powr-Pak conversions were made either at the NAPCO plants in Minneapolis and Detroit, at a participating Chevrolet dealership, or at other NAPCO distributorships. Chevy trucks dating back to 1942 could've been retrofitted, and the conversion was initially limited to three-quarter-ton models or larger due to the pre-1955 half-ton's incompatible torque-tube drive. Once the 1955 first-series pickup appeared in the fall of 1954 with a modern Hotchkiss-type driveshaft, the 4x4 switch was also made available for Chevy half-tons. By that time the typical NAPCO conversion added about $1,250 to the $1,550 spent on a typical Chevy half-ton. Along with the new-for-1955 half-ton inclusion came the possibility of a NAPCO-equipped panel truck or Suburban.

In any form, a NAPCO Chevrolet was more than capable of holding its own up against rival 4x4s of the day. As NAPCO brochures proudly put it: "Now you can have a standard Chevrolet four-wheel-drive pickup featuring the traction power of a tank, or, at the flip of a finger, a smoother riding, high speed, over the road truck. Aptly named the Mountain Goat, this full sized pickup will literally leap up mountains, as well as carry you through deep mud, sand, or snow."

Mountain Goat Chevy trucks performed so well they basically carried NAPCO right out of the picture. By 1956 GM officials had finally determined it was time to get into the 4x4 game. GM contracted NAPCO to supply its Powr-Pak kits directly to them, a new deal that allowed GMC that year to offer a "direct-from-the-factory" 4x4 option. When a similar option (RPO 690) appeared for Chevrolet trucks in 1957, it was limited to six-cylinder/four-speed models. In keeping with its "I'm-slightly-better-than-you" tradition, GMC 4x4 pickups from the beginning could've been ordered with a V-8 and an automatic transmission.

The factory price for a 3100-series 4x4 pickup in 1957 was $2,549—an obviously better bargain compared to the earlier NAPCO conversions. Chevrolet and GMC offered the NAPCO-supplied option in 1958 and 1959 before it cut ties completely with Minnesota. GM's new-for-1960 truck chassis with independent front suspension wasn't compatible with the existing Powr-Pak conversion; the job was no longer so quick and easy. Chevy and GMC 4x4 builders looked elsewhere for their components, and eventually began engineering the whole package themselves. By the end of the decade, the era of true factory-built four-wheel-drive Chevrolet/GMC pickups had begun.

As for NAPCO, it continued to carry on in fine fashion after GM ended relations in 1959, although it was no longer involved in the off-road business. Rights to the Powr-Pak conversion were sold to the Toledo-based Dana Corporation in the early 1960s. The named changed to NAPCO International in the 1980s, which by that time the firm had broadened its scope to include, among other things, communications equipment and aircraft spare parts. Today those Mountain Goat Chevys of 50 years ago represent dim, distant memories to a global company still on the rise.

While Chevrolet sold its early 4x4s direct from the factory, the all-important transfer case and related gear still came from the NAPCO people in Minnesota. NAPCO had been selling four-wheel-drive conversion kits to Chevy truck owners since just after World War II.

Right
The 3200-series pickup, a longer half-ton based on the three-quarter-ton pickup's 123.25-inch wheelbase, appeared in 1955. This 3200 "long-box" Chevy is a 1957 model. Notice the optional "big window" in back of the cab.

Below
Quad headlights, another trendy car-line design fad, carried over into Chevrolet pickup ranks in 1958. The Apache name (for half-ton models) also debuted that year.

windows pioneered by GM glassworks. As functional as it was trendy, the 1955 Chevy truck windshield opened up a truly wide field of vision for the driver. And that fabulous view grew even more impressive if the equally new Panoramic rear window was ordered. Total glass area measured 36 percent greater compared to 1954's cab when the big window option was added in 1955. Then only four slim (and obviously required) roof posts prevented a full 360-degree range of visibility.

Those four posts also contributed to what Chevrolet called its "load-pulling" look. Intentions here involved

complementing those car-line ties with purposeful, distinctively pickup-like impressions. The posts sloped forward to give the cab an image that hopefully compared to a team of horses leaning into the harness while tugging away at a heavy wagonload. Those headlight hoods complemented this forward-rake too, as did the rear fenders and wheel openings. Wheelhouses front and rear reflected a touch of aesthetics-conscious car-like style instead of looking like they had been hastily radiused out simply to allow clearance for the tires. A crisp lip further enhanced the artistic nature of those openings.

Additional breaks from previously popular truck trends included the deletion of running boards and the substitution of fully integrated fadeaway front fenders in place of those old-fashioned pontoons. Dodge had actually been the first to leave the past behind at each front corner in 1948 with the introduction of its B-series Pilot-House pickups. B-series fenders still stood out, but not nearly as much as previous fashions. They also weren't bulbous in the least, and they, too, stylishly faded away into the doors. Dodge refined this trendy look even further in 1954. Chevrolet then put its seal of approval on this front fender fad the following year. Ford, meanwhile, stuck with its old-style fat-fendered frontal impressions until 1957.

While Chevrolet rear fenders in 1955 carried on in the bolt-on pontoon tradition, they no longer looked like function-intensive afterthoughts, thanks to their

"load-pulling" shape. They were also further integrated into the overall image by way of a horizontal crease that carried over from the cab and front fenders.

The sum of these parts in 1955 represented one of the best balanced, most unified truck restyles ever seen to that point, with "one of the best" being the key term here.

Chevrolet wasn't the first to restyle its pickup front to back in slick new bodywork. In 1949 Studebaker had stepped out from the crowd with its own postwar milestone, an exceptionally good-looking truck that few today remember, basically because not that many customers noticed it 50 years ago.

Stepside Chevrolet pickups remained popular after the Fleetside appeared in 1958. Shown here is a 1959 Apache.

Only a new hood ornament and revised badging set the 1956 Chevy 3100 (left) apart from its 1955 forerunner. Task Force trucks were fitted with a new nose in 1958, featuring, most prominently, quad headlights. Shown on the right is a 1959 Fleetside Apache.

went one step beyond by eliminating the running boards normally found below all the other three-man-wide cabs rolling around in 1949.

Pickup buyers had never seen anything like it, but they would cast their eyes on something similar soon enough. Poor old Studebaker barely made a ripple in the light-truck market waters with its first modern postwar pickup. Yet, when big bully General Motors put its twist on Bourke's integrated theme six years later, its dominating truck division was instantly declared the industry's styling leader. Apparently might not only makes right, it also makes history.

Various factors delayed Chevrolet's latest historic introduction in the utility-vehicle field until March 25, 1955. The name this time for the division's new second-series models was "Task-Force Trucks." Resource-limiting

Far left
A traditional 1956 Stepside contrasts a flashy 1959 Fleetside—no need to specifically identify which is which.

Left
The Fleetside design was first created by Charles Jordan when he was dreaming up the Cameo Carrier. Ford then mimicked the look with its Styleside pickup in 1957. Chevrolet's first Fleetside then debuted midyear in 1958. Optional two-tone paint was introduced for the Fleetside in 1959.

Many of the options previously limited to car buyers began to appear on Task Force pickups after 1955, such as the prismatic traffic-light viewer.

That was unfortunate, because South Bend's 2R half-ton, the work of Loewy studio design genius Robert Bourke, was America's first fully styled truck. Unlike rival designers, Bourke concentrated on the image as a whole, not just the cab. While the Big Three's new postwar pickups featured attractive forms up front, they remained function-first in back. In each case, an age-old squared-off cargo box was plainly adorned with purposeful pontoons meant only to keep the mud down. In stark contrast, Studebaker's 1949 2R was handsomely styled from nose to tail in an unprecedented integral fashion. Bourke's sleek, clean cab was followed closely by rakish rear fenders that didn't look at all like afterthoughts. They were still pontoons, but they complemented instead of contrasted. And they came off every bit as modern looking as the rest of the truck. Bourke even

Many restorers erroneously paint Chevrolet's earliest truck V-8s to match their car-line cousins. But while it is known that Chevy truck V-8s were first painted grey, it may well have been possible for a passenger-car-engine paint job to find its way onto a pickup engine. The owner of this 1959 Chevy chose to use the so-called "incorrect" color you see here on this 283 V-8 while rebuilding this beauty because that's what showed up after close inspection of the reportedly untouched original engine block.

repercussions left over from Korean War restrictions and the extra effort needed to launch Chevrolet's new-for-1955 automobiles represented the two biggest reasons why the Task-Force line was so late for its coming-out party. All was forgiven, though, once these terrific-looking tough trucks went to work.

While the Task-Force look was certainly modern, some of its trendy image was a mirage of sorts. Like the 1949 Studebaker, the second-series Chevrolet truck for 1955 didn't actually come without running boards. At least not full ones. Those old familiar steps up into the cab were still there; they were just hidden inside the doors. And unlike Bob Bourke's clean classic, the 1955 Chevy pickup also retained another short running board section between the cab and each rear fender. It was this leftover vestige that would soon inspire a new model name: Stepside.

Beauty beneath the Task-Force pickup's skin included yet another improved steering system and longer leaf springs that reportedly made for an easier ride. Wheelbase was reduced one click to 115 inches to both help out in the weight distribution department and reduce the turning circle.

That new wheelbase, along with a widened front track, was the product of a redesigned ladder-type frame that indeed looked like a ladder from a plan view. The 1954 frame's side rails had widened out as they stretched backward: width was 26 inches at the front cross-member, 36 inches behind the engine, and 46 inches at the rear cross-member. Nineteen-fifty-five's perfectly parallel frame rails were a consistent 34 inches wide at all six cross-members. This new continuity translated into more room beneath the hood (for a V-8, no?), and it also conformed to an industry-wide width standard that specialty fleet suppliers followed when fitting bare-chassis models with purpose-built aftermarket bodies.

Almost lost within the 1955 Task-Force truck's widened engine bay was the familiar Thriftmaster six-cylinder, rated at 123 horsepower in standard form. The aforementioned 145-horse Trademaster V-8 was optional, and transmission choices numbered five: the base three-speed, a heavy-duty three-speed with or without overdrive, a four-speed manual, or the Hydra-Matic automatic. A modern 12-volt ignition system also appeared in 1955.

On the outside, paint choices were as wide as ever that year, further demonstrating the newfound attention to style. Thirteen solid shades were offered, along with 11 two-tone treatments for both Deluxe- and Standard-cab models. There was improved comfort and convenience as well, thanks to a collection of options that was even larger than 1954's. Along with V-8 power and all that extra glass, the 1955 light-duty list included, among other things, power steering and power brakes, features previously limited to heavy-truck customers. A big bright bird on the hood, car-style wheel covers, and baubles like door handle shields and an illuminated cigar lighter could be added for a nominal fee.

Needless to say, the attractive, even alluring Task-Force truck stayed atop industry sales rankings for all five years it was around, although Ford did actually manage to sell more light-duty pickups than Chevrolet in 1959. Styling updates during the 1955—1959 run typically involved revised trim and badges each year, and a restyled grille in 1957. The 1957 hood was also treated to twin windsplit sculpturing. Another new grille appeared in 1958 along with trendy quad headlights in place of the duals used previously.

All light trucks also began wearing Apache badges in 1958, but the real news involved the midyear introduction of the new Fleetside model. Featuring fully flush bodysides that ran back into a cab-wide cargo box, Chevrolet's Fleetside pickup grew from Chuck Jordan's 1953 Cameo sketches. Ford, too, added a little inspiration by copying the clean Cameo image in steel with its standard Styleside pickup in 1957. Chevrolet officials were left with little choice but to retool for a comparable rendition of the theme it had created in the first place. Once the more practical (and more affordable) steel-paneled Fleetside appeared early in 1958, the expensive (and fragile) fiberglass-bodied Cameo was cancelled. And Chevy's typical pickups—they with their typical pontoon fenders in back—then took on that aforementioned Stepside moniker.

The Fleetside attraction was heightened even further in 1959 with optional two-tone paint. That same year, Dodge jumped up on this stylish bandwagon with its first Sweptline pickup, which mercifully allowed Chrysler's truck division to retire its Cameo knock-off, the Sweptside, built from 1957–1959 using station-wagon rear quarterpanels to give it car-like impressions. This odd concoction could never quite compare to the Cameo.

Notable engineering advancements made during the Task-Force run included the introduction of Chevy's first factory-built four-wheel-drive pickup in 1957. While this rough-and-ready truck did rely on aftermarket components supplied by the NAPCO people in Minnesota, its out-sourced off-road equipment was installed on a Chevrolet assembly line, and the resulting product was then sold complete through a Chevy dealer. Off-road Buyers looking for the off-the-beaten-path before 1957 had to add the NAPCO "Mountain Goat" 4x4 conversion separately after taking delivery of a six-cylinder Chevrolet pickup based on a standard two-wheel-drive platform.

Improvements to that Thriftmaster six included a slight boost in power to 140 horses in 1956, then to 145 in 1958. The 265-ci Trademaster V-8 also grew to 155 horsepower in 1956. Chevrolet's enlarged 283-ci small-block then replaced the 265 on 1958's option list. Some sources (including apparently Chevy's own paperwork) claim the 283 had actually appeared late in 1957, the same year it debuted beneath automobile hoods. Nineteen-fifty-eight paperwork listed the Trademaster 283 at 160 horsepower. An optional four-barrel carburetor upped the output ante to 175 horses.

Ample power and a lot of style remained strong selling points for Chevrolet pickups as the 1950s closed. Nothing about these trucks looked "low-priced," save for those low prices themselves. "Best buy" was still a fair description—as it had been for 20 years.

A Star is Born
Carried Away by Cameo

Above
Chevrolet's new 1955 Task Force pickup was a looker on its own up front with its "egg-crate" grille and wraparound windshield. Standard Cameo touches included two-tone paint (available only in red-on-white that first year) and car-line full wheel covers.

Left
Chevrolet's Cameo Carrier first popularized the concept that a hard-working half-ton pickup could look every bit as classy as a car. Cameos were introduced in 1955 and cancelled in 1958. At left as a 1958 model, while at right is a 1956 Cameo.

In 1947 Chevrolet proved that pickups could be more comfortable and easier to drive, as well as easier on the eyes than prior vehicles suggested. Two years later Studebaker outdid anything Detroit had in the way of a good-looking truck, but few really noticed because . . . well, because Studebaker was Studebaker, an independent, not one of the Big Three prime-time players. Ford then rendered moot all previous claims to fame in 1953 by introducing the fabled F-100, a fine-looking pickup that offered even more comfort and convenience and was even more of a joy to operate. "Now top that!" surely must have been the battle cry around Dearborn that year.

Some historians today may consider the 1953 F-100 to be the milestone pickup of the postwar era, but in their day those fat-fendered Fords were quickly overshadowed by Chevrolet's best truck yet in 1955. Chevy's Task-Force models instantly made everything else that came before obsolete. Even though Ford designers by then were back at their drawing boards busily scribbling up a new-and-improved F-100 for 1957, they still couldn't top the truck that had everyone talking in 1955. And 1956. And 1957, 1958, and 1959.

To say that Chevrolet blew everyone away in the light-truck field in 1955 was akin to calling the sun warm. Those red-hot Task-Force trucks not only hauled away any hopes Dearborn dreamers had of retaking the industry's top spot, they also revved up additional momentum for the run into the next decade, which Chevy pickups again owned until Ford finally did find its way back to first in 1968. "What took you so long?" was probably the response heard most often around Chevrolet offices that year. Thirty years is a long, long time to chase a brass ring—just ask Chevy truck team members today.

Ford has since turned the table on Chevrolet, and America's best-selling truck will probably soon break the Bow-Tie record for most consecutive years leading the league. But if there's any consolation in the Chevrolet camp, it's the knowledge that Chevy trucks undoubtedly did more than any other rival during the 1950s to sow the seeds for the flourishing crop of user-friendly, completely classy, conveniently car-like utility vehicles that sell like hotcakes today. Granted, Ford laid a lot of the groundwork in 1953. It was then left to Chevrolet to raise the bar almost out of sight.

When those Task-Force trucks appeared in 1955, they were led by a flagship that, on its own, almost overnight changed the way Americans looked at their pickups. If any one vehicle can be called the main forerunner of today's multi-talented, truck-about-town utility vehicle, it is the glorious Cameo Carrier. At the least from an historical perspective, the Cameo certainly deserves equal billing alongside the 1953 F-100. But in many not-so-humble opinions, the former, not the latter, should rank as the milestone postwar pickup.

So what if the first F-100 transformed the old workhorse pickup into a daily driver? "Daily driver" was an insult to the elegant Cameo Carrier. Though it was very much a typical half-ton truck (albeit a Task-Force truck, then the richest kind) beneath that beautiful skin, it was the thick, sweet icing that made this all-too-common cake so irresistible. Giving greater attention to styling was one thing—a good-looking half-ton was nothing new in 1955—but creating a truly classy, if not downright classic, image was quite another, representing an unprecedented achievement in the utility-vehicle field.

The star, of course, of the Cameo show was its stylish cargo box, which was complemented with a "cleaned-up" tailgate, a unique rear bumper, and car-style taillights.

Above
The two-tone paint treatment carried over inside the cargo box. The tailgate's latches and lanyards were also unique to the Cameo.

Left
Creating the Cameo was so simple: off went those traditional "pontoon" fenders, on went attractive side panels molded out of fiberglass. The tailgate too was dressed up with a fiberglass cover.

Right
Right
The 1955 Cameo interior was also treated to a similar two-tone treatment. All Cameos were offered with automatic and manual transmissions and V-8 or six-cylinder power.

Far right
The Cameo appeared almost unchanged for 1956 save for the introduction of varying color choices. Also notice the small hubcaps with trim rings—both this look and full wheel covers were available.

This pretty pickup wasn't merely a progression, it stood head-and-shoulders above the rest as an all-new approach that left the past behind and redirected the future. The truck builder's focus immediately changed after the Cameo's appearance. Creating the most comfortable, convenient, easiest-to-handle trucks was no longer enough. These same utility vehicles had to be reasonably classy, too, almost as classy as cars. The Cameo may have ridden like a truck, driven like a truck, and, on occasion, worked like a truck. It nonetheless impressed nearly all critics with how well it could play like a car, something the American pickup wasn't allowed to do before 1955. Polite society let the Cameo into the club formerly limited only to cars because of this groundbreaking light truck's equally polite persona, which for the first time ever combined prestige with pickup

Although the Cameo was only around for four years, its prestigious presence is still felt today nearly a half-century later. Modern truck buyers are certainly spoiled; they automatically assume all pickups should turn heads like cars and play as hard as they work. It was Chevrolet that first conceived this concept in 1955.

Car-like style was the 1955 Cameo's forte, and a split personality only contributed to the attraction. This high-class half-ton looked right at home uptown or down on the farm. City slickers no longer feared being seen behind the wheel of—dare we say it?—a "pick-em-up truck." And country folk could be right proud of their Sunday-go-to-meetin' work truck.

Key to the Cameo's appeal was its trend-setting cargo box, a clean, classy shape initially sketched by Chuck Jordan. "It was about time to start the new truck program," recalled Jordan in a July 1977 interview with *Special Interest Autos* editor Michael Lamm. "We'd been anticipating the new truck with sketches that some of the other guys and I were doing in the studio. Lu [Stier] had given us enough time, we weren't that busy, so we could sit and do some advanced doodling."

Stier loved those "doodles," as did Chevrolet Chief Engineer Ed Cole. As he had done previously in the Corvette's case, Cole quickly gave his support to this new pickup project, and Stier's studio then got busy transforming Jordan's dream truck into reality.

"We worked late one night because we were going to have an important product policy meeting on the new truck program the next day," remembered Jordan in 1977. "We were all working hard by this time trying to figure out how to get this sleek-sided job sold. That night we finished a 3/8-scale illustration. It was really done around the cab that we were developing for the entire truck line. Reception to the design was so good that we decided to model it, and once it was modeled, there wasn't any question."

Around Chevrolet that design became known as the Fleetside. Unlike previous pickups, which featured typical cargo boxes sandwiched between two pontoon fenders in back, the original Fleetside body was based on a one-piece cab/bed arrangement that flowed uninterrupted from head to tail, per Jordan's specifications. Gone were those pontoons and steps behind the cab. In their place were cab-wide exterior bed walls that created clean, continuous bodysides comparable to the then-fresh slabside styling that was all the rage among automobile designers of the day.

Jordan's original scheme certainly was a head-turner, a plain truth clearly demonstrated by full-sized mockups. But Jim Premo, Cole's assistant, needed only one look at those mockups before casting a dark cloud over things. Integral cab/bed construction would never work in the real world, he concluded. Torsional stress on the frame would surely warp that super-smooth sheet metal at the point where the cab and cargo box met, an inherent reality that explained why all pickups had separate cabs and beds to begin with.

"At that point, the division was practically ready to abandon the idea, but our studio insisted we could separate the cab and box without losing the desirable exterior appearance," explained Lu Stier in another 1977 Mike Lamm interview. It was also then that Chevrolet bean counters determined the division couldn't afford at that time to produce the Fleetside cargo box out of steel. It did, of course, show up in all-steel form in 1958. By 1954, however, Chevrolet had already spent a bundle on the new Task-Force trucks to come; there simply was no cash left over for any additional trend-setting tangents.

Sexy Suburbanites

GMC's Cameo

GMC's version of the classy Cameo was called the Suburban Pickup. It, too, debuted in 1955 but was offered until 1959. Chevy's Cameo was cancelled in 1958. At right is one of GMC's rare 1955 Suburban Pickups; at left is an extremely rare 1959 model.

Getting lost in the shadow of its best-selling cousin has never necessarily been a bad thing for General Motors' "other" truck division. While Chevrolet had a stranglehold on number one for 30 years, GMC was down battling for fourth- or fifth-place with International. Beginning in 1954, the Dodge boys found themselves looking up at GMC and continued doing so until the mid-1960s.

By the 1950s, GMC had nurtured its own loyal customer base, a group big enough to keep GM's second truck line more than healthy—but not so big that it put a hurt on the corporation's first-and-foremost. Chevrolet sales never suffered in the least, not even while GMC trucks were being marketed as "a cut above." A little extra prestige—supplied mostly by a little extra chrome here and there—had supposedly set GMC pickups apart from their Chevy runing mates all along. "Upscale" power sources, first borrowed from Buick then Pontiac, also helped boost GMC's stock. But the primo pizzazz really began to pile on in March 1955.

Both corporate cousins shared that same snazzy second-series sheetmetal restyle, which looked awfully darn good that year wearing Chevrolet badges. GMC's truck team, however, just had to go one step beyond. Adding Pontiac's larger 287 cubic-inch overhead-valve V8 (which by the way pioneered the lightweight ball-stud rocker-arm setup that helped make Chevy's 265-cid small-block so hot) for the 1955 options list wasn't enough. Nor was "a little extra" prestige. Big, bold badges and an even bolder grille/bumper designer guaranteed that GMC's new pickups wouldn't end up lost in a crowd. Two huge chrome-encrusted grille bars reminded many critics of Oldsmobile's dramatic design unveiled a few years before. Others claimed they saw a touch of Cadillac in that pair of protruding "dagmars" on the bumper. Inside, a bright instrument panel plate dazzled drivers even further. Hands down, the 1955 GMC second-series trucks were the flashiest on the marekt that year, at leas far as "standard" models were concerned.

Chevrolet did have its lovely Cameo in 1955. Nothing from rival camps could compare to this beauty. But competition from within represented another story entirely. Those flush-mounted fibeglass panels found their way behind GMC cabs, too, resulting in the Suburban Pickupk, a Cameo copy that simply couldn't be missed. Car-style taillights and full wheel-covers, Panoramic glass front and rear, a spare tire cleverly hidden behind that stylish bumper in back—all the things that made Chevy's Cameo a classic were present and accounted for on GMC's Suburban Pickup, which some advertisements called a "Tennessee Hardtop."

The one main difference (there were many much more trivial design discrepancies) between the two involved color. Suburban Pickup buyers in 1955 were not limited to red-accented-white only. Any GMC paint scheme was available, as were a long list of options including GM's Hydra-Matic automatic transmission, power steering and brakes, a tachometer and a "space-age" vacuum-operated ashtray. Introduced for 1958, this self-cleaning butt-receptacle was, by most accounts, exclusive to GMC trucks. Apparently Chevrolet never offered it.

While the Cameo was updated in 1957 with new trim for its fiberglass cargo box panels, the GMC variant stayed with a "plain" box throughout its run. This 1958 Suburban Pickup features V-8 power and an optional sun visor.

GMC trucks used Pontiac powerplants during the 1950s. This is a 336-ci V-8 with a single four-barrel carburetor.

Chevrolet didn't offer a Cameo for 1959, either. GMC's Suburban Pickup did roll on into 1959, although production was surely quite low. Compared to the 5,000 Cameos buit for 1955-58, GMC reportedly put together barely 300 Suburban Pickups for its entire 1955-59 run. GMC designers also opted to stick with those original "plain" cargo box walls throughgat that run. Cameo pickups received new two-tone panels in back for 1957 and 1958. Accordingly Suburban Pickups never were treated to any special exterior identification. Chevrolet name-callers added "Cameo" script along with those contrasting cargo-box panels in 1957.

Even without specific badges, GMC's Suburban Pickups need no introduction on the rare occasions when they're sighted today. Few were built, far fewer remain. And not one has ever had any problem whatsoever finding the limelight.

"The cost of new tools and dies was too much for the projected low production volume," said Stier. Case closed? Not at all.

Jim Premo didn't shoot the project down; he simply explained to Stier's designers that the one-piece design would never float. Testing supported Premo's claim, but Jordan remained adverse to a typical cab/bed layout.

"We fought and fought and fought, and it wasn't a matter of economics so much as structure," said Jordan. "We wanted to keep the clean look of an integral cab and pickup box. But there was too much twist between the cab and the box, so we had to put in some clearance. It really hurt us to do that, but in retrospect it worked out all right."

That economic issue worked out all right as well. As the old joke goes, Chevrolet did have all that extra fiberglass lying around due to the fact that Corvette buyers were then staying away in droves. Why not just dress up the 1955 pickup's existing cargo box with fiberglass panels supplied by the same Moulded Fiberglass people who fabricate Corvette bodies in Ashtabula, Ohio? The solution appeared both simple and inexpensive—and workable.

"We were then able to convince the division that we could keep the existing stepside box and simply add fiberglass panels flush with the cab sides," continued Stier. "We also added a fiberglass cover to the existing tailgate." Saving extra costs by using the existing box structure as a skeleton also helped make the proposition "do-able." Sweetening the deal further was the fact that molding fiberglass was much cheaper than stamping steel, and those folks in Ashtabula then had nothing better to do.

Their latest handiwork ended up being the star of the Cameo show in 1955. Although a piece of chrome trim was required to distract attention away from the fact that there was still a gap between cab and bed, the Cameo's fiberglass cargo box coverings looked like they belonged there all along. Graceful, car-like wheel openings complemented the crisp, clean lines. Additional auto-style touches included distinctive taillights (that mimicked 1954 Bel Air units) and a unique rear bumper featuring a hinged center panel for access to the spare tire location beneath the rear bed floor. incorporated into the tailgate design were hidden hinges and latches and Nomad-like support cables in place of those typical chains. A big "Bow-Tie" badge in the center of that tailgate completed things.

Once the bed was made, putting the rest of the Cameo together was child's play. Chevrolet's 1955 cab redesign (also Jordan's work) already included a great-looking front end that, on its own, instantly reminded many witnesses of the division's even more historically significant redesigned 1955 automobiles. That egg-crate grille, those hooded headlights, and GM's trendy Panoramic wraparound windshield all worked in concert to guarantee that the front half of the Cameo wouldn't clash with that classy cargo box in back.

Remaining standard features included passenger-car full wheel covers and Chevrolet's various Custom Cab baubles: chrome grille and front bumper, a full-width Panoramic rear window, and extra brightwork inside and out. Powertrain choices were the same as the standard 3100-series line's. Cameo customers in 1955 had no choice whatsoever as far as the exterior paint scheme was concerned. An exclusive Bombay Ivory finish with Commercial Red cab accents was the only finish available that first year. Contrasting red paint also carried over inside the cargo box.

Accents and styling queues weren't the only things car-like about the Cameo Carrier. A six-cylinder, two-door Bel Air hardtop carried a base price of $2,067 in 1955. Introduced in March that year, the first Cameo's bottom line was commonly quoted at about $2,000, around 30 percent more than a typical Chevy pickup cost in those days. That figure alone would have been enough to send most truck buyers home with their pockets turned inside out. But Chevrolet commonly delivered Cameos to dealers loaded with options with the intention of further heightening an already high profile vehicle. Typical price tags reportedly surpassed $3,000.

Buyers, however, barely blinked an eye. Cameo production in 1955 totaled 5,220, a comparatively tidy figure that looked reasonably large, considering the vehicle's narrow niche. Sales then predictably declined as the novelty wore off and those high prices hit home.

Cameo production dropped to 1,452 in 1956 for a second-edition model that was basically identical (save for typical trim updates) to the first. The big news that year was the arrival of optional paint schemes, eight in

all. Joining the familiar two-tone combo, now called Bombay Ivory and Cardinal Red, were Cardinal Red/Sand Beige, Golden Yellow/Jet Black, Cardinal Red/Arabian Ivory, Regal Blue/Arabian Ivory, Granite Grey/Arabian Ivory, Ocean Green/Arabian Ivory, and Crystal Blue/Arabian Ivory.

Sales revived in 1957 when the Cameo was treated to chrome-trimmed contrasting panels for those fiberglass box walls in back. "Cameo" script, located in the forward portions of those panels, also appeared for the first time. And paint choices increased to nine: Ocean Green/Bombary Ivory, Cardinal Red/Bombay Ivory, Indian Turquoise/Bombay Ivory, Alpine blue/Bombay Ivory, Sand Beige/Bombay Ivory, Golden Yellow/Jet Black, Granite Grey/Bombay Ivory, Bombay Ivory/Cardinal Red, and Sandstone Beige/Bombay Ivory. Total production in all colors was 2,244.

There were nine colors again in 1958, although the combos varied slightly: Dawn Blue/Marine Blue, Polar Green/Jade Green, Tartan Turquoise/Jet Black, Kodiak Brown/Bombay Ivory, Oriental Green/Bombay Ivory, Granite Grey/Bombay Ivory, Cardinal Red/Bombay Ivory, Bombay Ivory/Cardinal Red and Golden Yellow/Jet Black. Production hit 1,405 before Chevrolet officials decided to close down the Cameo show in the middle of the production year. Ford had begun offering its standard Styleside pickup the year before, and Chevrolet's appropriately named Fleetside was then waiting in the wings as a more affordable response for 1958. So, it was out with the high-priced, comparatively fragile fiberglass-bodied Cameo, and in with the all-steel, better-suited-for-the-mainstream Fleetside.

Though killed early in 1958, the Cameo was by no means a disappointment. Success in this case shouldn't be measured by sales figures or longevity; it is defined better by impact. Plainly put, the pickup market was never the same again after the Cameo's debut. Chevrolet had clearly demonstrated what a little (or a lot of) car-like class could do for pickup popularity, and that demonstration was not lost on rival truck makers.

Nearly 50 years later we are all reaping rewards resulting from that ongoing competition. The next time you take your place behind the wheel of whatever brand sport-truck, sport-ute, or whatever you drive, perhaps you could thank the Cameo—and Chevrolet.

Far left top
All Cameo's featured this clever spare tire storage area hidden behind the rear bumper's center section. Shown here is the 1958 application.

Far left middle
A floor-shifter in the 1950s signified the presence of the heavy-duty four-speed with its low, low first gear—an odd option for the Cameo in 1958, considering the little-work, mostly play aspect of this model.

Far left bottom
An enlarged small-block V-8, the 283 was new for 1958, with a four-barrel carb feeding fuel-air. The 283 was mentioned for late 1957 Chevrolet pickups; installations were apparently rare.

Sweptsides *Swept Away*

Dodge's Sweptside pickup was created by grafting station wagon rear-quarter sheet metal right onto a pickup cargo box. This "Cameo wannabe" was introduced in May 1957.

Americans couldn't help but look at light-trucks differently after the Cameo came along. Both Ford and International-Harvester pickup planners were inspired by Chevrolet's trendy styling touches and unveiled copycat cosmetic makeovers for their half-tons in 1957. In each case, the main attraction was yet another cab-wide cargo box that eliminated the pontoon fenders. Cutting-edge looks with clean, crisp lines became the craze almost overnight as truck marketeers discovered there was absolutely nothing wrong with combining the practicality of a pickup with some of the automobile's class. Dearborn designers in 1957 took this fresh concept even furtherand created the Ranchero, an attractive, easy-to-handle utility vehicle that was part pickup, part car.

Not to be left behind, the guys at Chrysler's truck division also tried a little Cameo-copying in 1957 because they were willing to try anything. Dodge pickup sales fell each year as the 1950s progressed. Dodge trucks had claimed a solid 15.43 percent of the market in 1946, and they were still healthy in third-place in 1952 with 12.58 percent of the pie, but there was a decline. Dodge dropped behind International into fourth in 1953, and then slipped another notch below GMC the following year. The so-called third member of the Big Three remained stuck in the truck industry's fifth position for the remainder of the decade.

The reason why Dodge fell into this slide was somewhat of a mystery, especially to the division's designers and engineers, who had done so many things right with the new postwar pickups. In 1948 Dodge had become the first to adjust chassis geometry to make its trucks easier to drive. The division then jumped into the lead of the pickup power pack in 1954 with its first V-8. Apparently it was better to look good than to run well. Dodge pickups were sound beneath the skin, but simply couldn't compete as far as style and flair were concerned at the time.

Two years later Dodge hit the market with a stylish half-ton of its own. It was a somewhat odd concoction that one-upped the Cameo when it came to car-like impressions. Introduced in May 1957, Dodge's D100 Sweptside pickup literally was half truck, half car. Up front, it wore Dodge's newly restyled light-truck nose, a shape influenced by Chrysler designer Virgil Exner and his "Forward Look." In back, it traded pontoon fenders for a clean, uncluttered cab-wide cargo box. Instead of fiberglass fabrication, Dodge's quick-thinkers were able to use the existing steel body panels to avoid any excessive retooling costs.

The simple plan came from the fertile mind of Joe Berr, manager of the truck line's Special Equipment Group, an independent shop that operated freely within the Dodge organization to help meet special requests for custom-built vehicles not offered through customary channels. Berr and his team worked free of bureaucratic red tape; they didn't need upper management approval for any particular project or special order.

Thusly unhindered, Berr began his quest to beat Chevrolet at its own game and pulled a 116-inch wheelbase D100 pickup into his shop and removed the rear fenders. He then made a trip to Dodge's main assembly plant where he copped a pair of quarter-panels right off of a 1957 Suburban two-door station wagon. While he was there, he also grabbed the Suburban's rear bumper. Berr handed these Dodge car parts to SEG man Burt Nagos, who welded the Suburban sheetmetal, complete with its high-flying fins and "signal tower" taillights, to the D100 pickup's cargo box.

That snazzy station wagon bodywork fit like a glove, as did the rear bumper. Tying things together was as easy as adding a little extra trim to the cab to match the Suburban's existing two-tone layout. The only tough job was to cut down the D100's tailgate to fit between the two towering fins. The resulting gate (with hand latches in place of the typical chain hooks) was a bit crude, but the budget Berr and his team had was next to nothing.

Two-tone paint, full wheelcovers, and a chrome-plated front bumper to match the rear completed the package. "Straight out of tomorrow" bragged brochures about the 1957 Sweptside, although this high-profile half-ton remained quite familiar to truck buyers who weren't wowed by its cross-dressing nature. While a decent list of options could spruce things up, a standard Sweptside was still very much a spartan Dodge pickup inside and underneath.

Standard power came from Dodge's yeoman 230-ci L-head six-cylinder rated at 120 horsepower. The company's 314-ci "Powerdome" V-8—ranked as the light-truck market's strongest engine at 204 horsepower—was a $105 option. Additional extra-cost items included Dodge's pushbutton-controlled Loadflite three-speed automatic transmission, power steering and brakes, Custom Cab dress-up features, and wide-whitewall tires.

Although it turned heads, the Sweptside pickup did little to help reverse the division's sagging sales. Dodge's flashiest light-truck reappeared in similar fashion (with new Dodge sheetmetal up front) in 1958 was quietly discontinued in 1959. It was quickly forgotten, just like so many other fad-conscious flights of fancy from the 1950s.

Dodge built a few Sweptside pickups in 1959 before giving up on this odd concoction.

When Car Met Truck

The El Camino Hits the Road

Above
Chevrolet finally began offering an SS 396 El Camino in 1968. Production that first year was 5,190.

Left
Chevrolet discontinued its full-size El Camino after 1960, then returned in 1964 with a redesigned mid-sized rendition based on the new A-body Chevelle.

The concept was nothing new no matter how loudly ad copy bragged that it was. Mating car with truck had been tried before Chevrolet announced its intriguing El Camino to the world late in 1958. And no, we're not talking about Ford's Ranchero, the intriguing dual-purpose machine introduced for 1957. The real roots of the concept run back to the pickup's earliest days.

As was the case at Ford and Dodge, Chevrolet's first commercial vehicles were all cars morphed into trucks. And if that Model 490 half-ton delivery in 1918 was too much truck for you, there were Chevrolet's roadster pickups of the 1920s with slip-in cargo boxes in their trunks. These odd-looking concoctions survived into the 1930s, when they were joined by a new roadster pickup that truly was half car, half truck, not just a Chevy automobile with a box stuffed up its rear. From the front it looked like a car. The view from the back, however, was pure pickup thanks to the addition of a real half-ton truck bed.

Though GM's low-priced division built its last roadster pickup in 1932, the idea of a car-truck hybrid simply wouldn't go away. Chevy's creative crew dusted off the "box-in-a-trunk" idea in 1936—this time applying it to business coupes—and their "coupe pick-up" remained a relative success right up to World War II. It at least represented enough of a blip on rival radar screens to bring competitive forces into action. Plymouth, Ford, Hudson, and Studebaker all copied the concept.

Far right
Far right
Chevrolet's first El Camino was basically a two-door station wagon with its rear roof section removed. Sales in 1959 surpassed 22,000, compared to the 14,100 Rancheros built by Ford that year.

Below
Though Ford was first with its Ranchero, Chevrolet's copy, the El Camino, was far more successful. Total El Camino sales for 1959 to 1988 doubled the Ranchero output of 1957–1979. The 1959 El Camino on the right is joined by a 1986 model to clearly demonstrate the difference a quarter-century can make.

Before Studebaker created its coupe-pickup in 1940, the veteran independent auto maker from Indiana had borrowed a page out of Hudson's book. Hudson's first pickup, introduced in 1934, truly was half-and-half: automobile sheet metal was simply lopped off right behind the seat, and a pickup-style cargo box was bolted on in back of the grafted-on rear cab wall. Studebaker's first pickup was created the same way in 1937 using a Dictator passenger car. The resulting Coupe Express continued to carry the load up through 1939. Hudson, meanwhile, kept its hybrid hauler up and running into 1947—long enough to leave memories fresh when the Ranchero made the scene 10 years later.

Dearborn designers clearly had a little outside help in the inspiration department. GM product planners then were handed the "car-truck" idea on a silver platter.

It was simply too good to pass up, but you would have thought that Chevy's copycats might have preferred a less obvious approach. Even the name they chose for their Ranchero knock-off mimicked the Ford's south-of-the-border-sounding moniker.

Spanish/English dictionaries inform us that "El Camino" means "the road," a long and winding one in this case. Chevy's car-truck may have been a copy, but how could anyone dismiss a coat-tailer that ended up selling so well for so many years? Though the Ranchero was first, it was El Camino owners who got the last laugh after Ford finally closed the tailgate on its hybrid in 1979. Chevrolet's car-truck survived another nine years before arriving at trail's end. Official production ended with only 420 El Caminos built for 1988.

The El Camino enjoyed 27 model runs versus 23 for the Ranchero. Eagle-eyed readers might notice that things don't quite add up on the El Camino's side of the equation—this is because Chevy's 27 years were not consecutive like Ford's. El Camino production temporarily ceased after 1960 while GM geniuses went back to their drawing boards after watching Ford repackage its Ranchero that year as a compact Falcon. Dearborn's daredevils had tested shark-infested market waters first, then decided to come back ashore for a smaller boat once popularity of their original full-sized model began to sink. Although fortunes did resurface in 1959 (after nose-diving in 1958), the third-edition Ranchero still was no match for the new El Camino, which outsold its incumbent rival by nearly 60 percent. But downsizing instantly turned the tables. The first Falcon Ranchero beat Chevy's second El Camino the following year by nearly the same margin, making it the only time Ford would win the car-truck race. And Chevrolet's truck builders didn't take too kindly to losing.

Falcon Rancheros had the market all to themselves in 1961, 1962, and 1963 after the Bow-Tie boys seemingly took their ball and stomped all the way home. In truth, Chevrolet officials were regrouping, rethinking their position. They didn't have anything else to work with, at least not until 1964, when General Motors' new A-body intermediates debuted. A Chevelle-based mid-sized El Camino then became just the ticket to help usher Ford back into second place.

Second-generation El Camino sales were nearly double of its pint-sized rival every year during the 1960s, and Ford didn't regain much ground after moving the Ranchero into intermediate-size ranks in 1967. Rancheros never came close during the 1970s, and the score grew even more lopsided after GMC rolled out its El Camino running mate, the Sprint, in 1971. The Sprint was then superseded in 1978 by the repackaged Caballero, which, like the El Camino, carried on in ever-decreasing numbers until 1988. GMC's final production tally of the Sprint that year was a mere 325.

The El Camino's zenith came in 1973, when production soared to 64,987. GMC that year sold a record 6,766 Sprints. The Caballero topped out at 6,952 units in 1979, the same year Ford men watched their last Ranchero roll out the door. Chevrolet beancounters

Far left
A wide range of power sources were available for the first El Camino, including everything from frugal six-cylinder to the fire-breathing triple-carb 348 big-block V-8. Shown here is the 283-ci small-block.

Left
True to the pickup side of its alter ego, the 1959 El Camino's standard interior was a plain-Jane place in which to drive.

little pickup practicality yet still demanding certain levels of convenience, class, and style. Image-conscious businesses serving high-placed clientele—people who tended to look down their noses at a truck parked in their circle drive—were also targeted.

Indeed, throughout its career the El Camino represented more icing than cake. Most served their masters best in figurehead roles, looking right fine with a company logo stuck on the door while the boss toured the jobsite hauling nothing more than a hardhat, a coffee jug, and a bad temper. Even with optional heavy-duty suspensions or towing packages, the El Camino's car-line heritage still limited it mostly to recreational uses and household-type chores. Pulling a ski boat or moving your worthless brother-in-law's furniture (a well-worn Lazy-Boy and concrete-block shelving) from one studio apartment to the next was about as far down the hauling road as the half-truck went.

Beyond that, many customers simply chose an El Camino as attractive, everyday transportation, with little or no thought of ever putting it to work. Why not? Any El Camino could turn nearly as many heads as its passenger-car counterpart, while always standing ready should a stray washer and/or dryer want for transportation to a new home. And when fully loaded down with options, Chevy's car-truck also stood on its own as a certified status machine complemented by all the bells and whistles. By the time the 1970s arrived, no one was questioning how such frivolities as vinyl roofs, air conditioners, and 8-track players (playing Jimi Hendrix's *Purple Haze* perhaps?) fit into that equation, a paradoxical formula that supposedly involved a yeoman-like, salt-of-the-earth utilitarian variable too. Even hot performance could be thrown into the mix. It was clear that the El Camino was never meant to be all-work, no play. It was the vehicle's playfulness that made it so popular.

But such popularity remained a bit iffy in the beginning. As mentioned, melding with the marketplace was a matter of time and testing for both Ranchero and El Camino. Ford officials learned early on that bigger wasn't necessarily better, because really big loads weren't what potential buyers wanted to carry. Spending big money apparently wasn't in the plans, either. The Ranchero survived into the 1960s only because it was repackaged in its more affordable, much more compact

soon found themselves watching El Camino sales drop steadily during the 1980s until the market finally fully dried up. In the end the copy outsold the original by a 2-1 score. If you include the 36,576 Sprints and 37,719 Caballeros from GMC, the all-time El Camino tally for its 27-year run was 1,056,424. Ford's 23-year total was about 508,000.

And to think the whole car-truck craze basically had begun on a whim. There was no way Ford men in 1957 could have been sure there would actually be a demand for a car that could do at least some of the work of a truck. Did buyers then really want (or need) to walk the fence between automobile and pickup? Or did the first Rancheros and El Caminos represent the tail wagging the dog? Were the two simply the newest curiosities in a long line of 1950s fantasies, vehicles that made it on the scene only because they inspired fad-conscious customers to be the first on their blocks to jump on Detroit's latest, greatest trendy bandwagon?

Any worries at Ford concerning how skeptics would respond to this new multi-roller were surely eased by the plain fact that it would be so easy (and cheap) to build. Just cut the roof off a station wagon; a tailgate was already in place. Start-up costs were minimal, so Ford basically couldn't lose, even if a solid market failed to form.

Chevrolet officials were a bit more specific when describing a target market for the new El Camino two years later. According to Assistant General Sales Manager Albert Olson, Jr., Chevy's answer to the Ranchero also responded to a newfound need on the West Coast for a comfortable pickup. In Olson's humble opinion, potential customers were wealthy, higher-brow buyers looking for a

Above
The second-generation El Camino's base six-cylinder engine in 1964 was a 120-horse, 194-ci powerplant. The 155-horsepower 230-ci High-Thrift six was optional.

Right
Beginning in 1965, all the same features found on the SS 396 Chevelle were available at extra cost to El Camino buyers, but customers couldn't add any of the SS nomenclature. Although this sporty 1967 El Camino bucket seat/console interior looks every bit like that of its SS 396 running mate, nowhere can any "SS" references be found.

Falcon form. Once established at the right size and price, both hybrid rivals immediately found a niche. Long careers then followed.

The El Camino's stint officially began on October 16, 1958. From the cab down it was pure 1959 Chevrolet, with the obvious addition of the bed in back. Rear-quarter sheet metal and tailgate came from the two-door Brookwood station wagon, the long sidespear was a Bel Air piece, and those high-flying fins were seemingly not of this Earth. The running joke at Ford that year was that Chevrolet's new body resembled a Martian ground chariot. Even styling chief Claire MacKichan later admitted that "we just went farther than we should have." MacKichan's team traveled the farthest with those horizontal fins, called bat wings by many. Nonetheless, you had to admit that 1959 Chevys did turn heads wherever they went—on this planet or any other.

More than one critic actually liked the way Chevrolet's out-of-this-world 1959 sheet metal fit the first El Camino. According to a May 1959 *Motor Life* review, those "gull wing fins blend in with the pickup bed better, perhaps, than they do with any other body style in the Chevy line." *Motor Life's* judge and jury also felt Chevrolet designers outdid their Ford counterparts: "While the El Camino resembles a passenger car in every way, except for the short cab and stylish pickup bed, even the cab has rakish lines—more so than the Ranchero inasmuch as the rear window is not squared off but has a graceful forward slope."

The first-generation Ranchero definitely appeared like a quick-fix due to its sawed-off cab. The 1959 El Camino's cab, in comparison, came off as an integral styling element. Its distinctive overhanging roof and sloping, wraparound glass in back mimicked the flyaway roofline of Chevrolet's four-door Impala Sport Sedan. Minimal posts at the corners and a huge compound-curve windshield up front accentuated the airy greenhouse image.

Beneath the skin was Chevrolet's rigid X-member chassis with coil springs at all four corners, a design introduced for 1958. El Camino updates included station wagon rear springs and shocks, while all 1959 Chevys got a revamped rear suspension featuring a new upper control arm layout, an additional frame cross-member, and a lateral anti-sway bar. A typical 1959 El Camino was still softly sprung, a concession to the passenger-car side of its split

Performance played a major part in the El Camino's progress through the 1960s and 1970s. The SS 454 El Camino appeared in 1970 armed with either the LS-5 or LS-6 Mk IV big-block V-8. Perhaps the greatest performance powerplant built during the musclecar era, the rare LS-6 El Camino was a 450-horsepower screamer. This is the tamer LS-5 SS 454.

Ranchero | Deja Vu *All Over Again*

Ford built its last Ranchero in 1979. Total production for the breed dating back to 1957 was about 500,000.

Detroit decision-makers never have been shy about copying another's work and claiming it as their own. When the El Camino appeared for 1959, Chevrolet hype-masters had the gall to call it "the brightest new idea of the year." New idea? Where were they when the same lightbulb had lit up above Dearborn designers' heads a few years before? Most people could see that the El Camino was an obvious knock-off of one of Ford's better ideas.

Introduced to the American public in November 1956, Ford's first Ranchero had actually re-introduced the American public to the concept of a car that could work like a truck. Or was it a truck that could play like a car? Either way, this curious concoction wasn't exactly the first of its breed, especially considering that nearly all of the Big Three's earliest trucks were cars fitted with heavier springs and harder-working bodies. Ford managed to mate car and truck together in a far superior fashion to anything that had come before. The Blue Oval gang did the job so well, their arch-rivals at Chevrolet simply had to follow suit or lose face forever.

Chevy's clever designers even repeated the same simple trick that Ford designers had pulled out of their bag to create the first of the modern car-truck breed. Like the Ranchero, Chevrolet's 1959 copycat was not much more than a two-door station wagon with its rear roof area chiseled away to reveal the pickup-style cargo box hidden within. Michelangelo would've been proud.

According to Ford promotional literature, the 1957 Ranchero was "America's first work or play truck." It was marketed as a half-ton pickup among the company's truck line, but it clearly looked and handled a lot like a car.

Except for heavier springs, it was basically all car beneath its skin. The first Ranchero shared its tailgate, rear compartment sub-floor, and wheelbase with Ford's 1957 two-door Ranch Wagon. Obvious differences included the truncated roofline and pickup bed. Stampings for the roof, upper cab panel, double-walled cargo box, bed floor, and tailgate inner panel were unique to the Ranchero.

Impressions were equally unique. "For the person who has always wanted a pickup, but is balked by the looks or ride qualities inherent in normal trucks, Ford has come to the rescue," announced a *Motor Life* review. As a pickup it could haul upwards of 1,190 pounds in its 32.4 cubic-foot cargo box. As a car it could be dressed down with almost every comfort and convenience option offered by Ford in 1957, including power steering and brakes, air conditioning, electric seats and windows, and Signal-Seek radio. A V-8 engine and the Ford-O-Matic automatic transmission were also available at extra cost. Even the Thunderbird's 312-ci V-8, which early in the year could've been fitted with optional dual four-barrel carburetors or a supercharger, was a 1957 Ranchero option. All this potential pizzazz, performance, and practicality wrapped up in one package was too much for *Motor Trend's* Walt Woron to resist. In his words, the first Ranchero featured "the room and 'personal' feel of a Thunderbird, the comfort of a sedan, and the load-carrying capacity of a small pickup."

Production of the first Ranchero hit 20,000, and was more than enough to convince Dearborn execs to keep it around for a while. Its continued popularity proved that the car-truck combination definitely was a better idea. The Ranchero brought a steady stream of customers through 1979. The El Camino took a rest between 1961 and 1963.

Like the El Camino, the Ranchero experienced more than one transformation during its 23-year career. In 1960 it was reintroduced as a variation on Ford's all-new compact Falcon theme, a petite role it played reasonably well up through 1966. Ranchero then became a Fairlane offering in 1967 and jumped up a notch into Dearborn's intermediate ranks where it stayed through evolutions as a Torino-based model (until 1977), followed by an LTD II variant for its last three renditions. Total production for 1957–1979 was 508,355: 45,814 first-generation versions, 139,694 Falcon-based models, and 322,847 of the remaining versions. Again like the El Camino, the Ranchero hit its peak in 1973 when 45,741 models were sold.

Ranchero's roots run back to the early 1950s when a Ford designer drew up a new proposal as part of his company's 1952 model-line restyle. These sketches mimicked Ford of Australia's popular "Ute," a half-breed utility vehicle that had been beating the bush "down under" since the 1930s. Around Dearborn, the name for this Ute spin-off became the "Roo Chaser." Although the idea was first turned down, the Roo Chaser idea eventually resurfaced after Robert McNamara took over as Ford Division general manager early in 1955.

The Ranchero was then rushed to market for 1957, and Walt Woron couldn't resist making a reasonably obvious conclusion: "I'll go on record with a proclamation that the Ranchero will be copied in principle by other manufacturers. It's too good to pass up."

THE RANCHERO MODELS

The Ranchero: Bright-metal windshield, back window and vent wing moldings; bright-metal grille and front and rear bumpers standard. Single Colors: choice of Raven Black, Dresden Blue, Starmist Blue, Colonial White, Cumberland Green, Willow Green, Silver Mocha, Doeskin Tan, Woodsmoke Gray, Gunmetal Gray and Flame Red. Upholstery: choice of tan-and-brown woven plastic with tan vinyl bolster . . . or blue vinyl with white bolster. Engines: 144-hp 223 Six or 190-hp 272 V-8. Max. GVW 4,600 pounds.

Custom Ranchero includes all brightwork of the Ranchero, plus bright-metal cap molding around top of body and rear of cab . . . and distinctively different bright-metal full length side moldings. Available in all Single Colors (above) or in stunning Style Tone—Colonial White above side moldings, with any of the other ten colors below side moldings and on cab roof. Upholstery: choice of four combinations with white vinyl facings and bolsters—tan and brown or white and blue woven plastic, all red or all green vinyl. Engines: 144-hp 223 Six or 212-hp 292 V-8. Max. GVW 4,600 pounds.

rd's first Ranchero was created basically by sawing the rear roof section off of a 1957 Ranch Wagon. Full-sized Rancheros were built until 1959.

personality. Body roll was considerable in the turns, and load capacity wasn't all that great. *Motor Life* reported a noticeable squat with 700 pounds of cargo in back, more than enough weight to bottom out the suspension even over the smallest of bumps. Although heavier springs were available at extra cost, the trade-off was a distinctive forward rake, a nose-down position pickup owners were well acquainted with but a stance not all car buyers wanted.

Pickup buyers, on the other hand, probably didn't think much of the 1959 El Camino's price. A typical Stepside Chevy half-ton cost about $1,950 that year, compared to $2,500 for its car-truck cousin. A long list of options was also offered to hike the El Caminos bottom line even higher. Like its rival from Ford, the first El Camino was available with almost every passenger-car feature, including power brakes and steering, two-tone paint, deluxe interior appointments, and so on.

Powertrain choices included everything available to your average 1959 Impala buyer, from the basic 235-ci thrifty six-cylinder, to the 283-ci small-block V-8, all the way up to the hot-blooded 348 "W-head" big-block with

or without triple carburetion. Transmission choices were equally wide, beginning with the standard three-speed manual. Overdrive, a four-speed with a floor-shifter, and the two automatics—Powerglide and Turboglide—waited just one optional check-off away.

Performance, pizzazz, practicality—the El Camino offered it all, apparently more so than the 1959 Ranchero. Sales that year totaled 22,246 for the Chevrolet, 14,169 for the Ford. Then the shine came off Chevy's new toy. Second-edition El Camino production for 1960 fell by 37 percent to 14,163. Discounting the 1987–1988 encore, this figure represented the lowest production total put up by the El Camino during its long, long haul. It was also the last score registered until 1964.

The original El Camino's fate was surely decided even before the radically downsized Ranchero arrived in 1960. Creating a car-truck based on Chevrolet's passenger-car platform in 1959 and 1960 had been a piece of cake, relatively speaking. The job would have been nowhere near as easy using the redesigned 1961 Chevy as a foundation. Nor did the company's new compact, the Corvair, qualify, because of its rear engine. Modifying the unit-body Chevy II was briefly considered but quickly ruled out, leaving Chevrolet officials no choice but to wait until the new Chevelle debuted for 1964.

Although technically a notch lower than its ancestor in Chevy's new five-tiered model-line pecking order, the 1964 El Camino still ranked right up with its full-sized forefather in all the important categories. Weight and wheelbase were both down, but the cargo box was actually larger in height and length, and maximum payload was listed as 1,200 pounds. Base price (with a six) was $2,267; adding the 283-ci V-8 upped the ante by $100. Upscale Custom models were also offered with either power source, and they justified their higher price ($80 more) with added style and class.

Available with every option (save for the Super Sport package) that helped make the Chevelle such a sensation right out of the box, the A-body El Camino emerged as a sexy, sporty, sensible solution to the problem of how to have your cake and eat it too. Buyers loved Chevrolet's repackaged dual-purpose hybrid to death, both for how great it looked and how hard it worked. Chevrolet sold 36,615 that first year, more than twice the number of 1964 Rancheros unloaded by Ford.

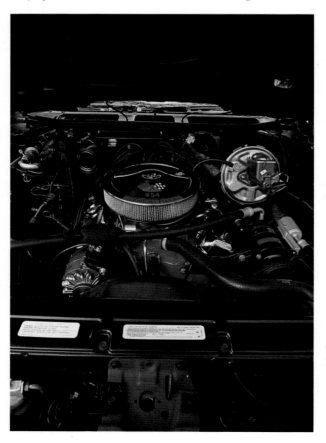

The LS-5 454 V-8 was rated at 360 horsepower in 1970. Compression was 10.25:1.

Above
Sporty five-spoke wheels, appropriate badging, and a "power bulge" hood were all included in the SS package in 1970. Both the SS 396 and SS 454 were offered that year.

Left
Another restyle for the Chevelle platform in 1973 resulted in a remade El Camino that year. The 1973 El Camino was the most popular of the breed—sales that year soared to nearly 65,000.

CHAPTER SIX

Right
GMC introduced its own El Camino, the Sprint, in 1971. Shown here is a 1974 model. The Sprint was superseded by the Caballero in 1978.

The Chevelle/El Camino platform was downsized for 1978 in the best interests of less weight and greater fuel efficiency. El Camino production that year remained healthy at 54,286.

The El Camino fan base grew as more and more performance and pizzazz filtered into the mix. By 1966 almost everything the Chevelle SS offered to musclecar buyers, including the hairy 396-ci Mk IV big-block V-8, rated as high as 375 horsepower, had become an El Camino option. Exceptions again included the famous Super Sport nomenclature itself. In 1966 and 1967 the Mk IV big-block was only available to Chevelle customers as part of the SS 396 performance package. El Camino customers could

order the 396—as well as bucket seats, a console, and the SS 396's mag-style wheel covers—but the SS imagery was unavailable.

That changed in 1968 when Chevrolet finally began offering an SS 396 El Camino complete with the revered "SS 396" badging, blacked-out grille, and bulging hood. Production for the first Super Sport El Camino was 5,190, helping total El Camino sales shoot up by 20 percent to a new high of 41,791. A similar sales jump followed in 1969, with the final tally soaring to 48,385.

El Caminos didn't come much flashier than the Royal Knight rendition, introduced in 1981. Gold-accented black paint helped guarantee you couldn't miss this one parked outside the disco.

Maximum performance then soared too in 1970 as the SS 454 option debuted for both the Chevelle and El Camino. Most SS 454 El Caminos that year featured the 360-horse LS-5 454 big-block. A meager few were actually ordered with the 450-horsepower LS-6 454, considered by many to be the most intimidating powerplant ever to roast a tire tread during the musclecar era. By 1968 it was obvious that work had given way to play in the car-truck field. "El Camino and Ranchero have established a new trend in the fun car market, and people all over the country are getting on the bandwagon," wrote Lee Kelley in a December 1967 *Motorcade* report.

With or without a fire-breathing engine under the hood, Chevy's car-truck remained a hot seller into the 1970s and was a common sight on or off the road. In truth, performance-conscious customers made up only one small faction among the El Camino faithful, and sales continued running stronger than ever, even after the horsepower race all but died out in 1972. Aided by a complete makeover for the Chevelle shell, the El Camino hit its peak the following year, surpassing the previous new sales high established in 1972. By 1973, vehicles Chevrolet considered mid-sized had grown every bit as large and heavy as the cars used as bases for the original El Caminos of 1959–1960. That wasn't a bad thing—it was what customers wanted. Added girth meant added room and comfort. Added style and class just came along as part of the deal, as more size meant extra room for additional options.

Ford's Ranchero also peaked in 1973 then quickly faded, thanks in part to the gas crunch. Chevrolet sold twice as many El Caminos each year thereafter until the Better Idea guys finally plugged the plug in 1979. Chevy built 58,008 El Caminos that year, the model's second highest year-end total. Still a very popular, very sporty utility vehicle in the late 1970s, especially in its ever-present SS trim, the El Camino, along with its Caballero cousin from GMC, just wouldn't let up. And designers kept creating ever flashier dress-up packages, including the disco-safe Royal Knight and Diablo models, introduced by Chevrolet and GMC, respectively, in 1978. Another restyle, this one reverting back to lighter, leaner lines, also came that year.

Running alone into the 1980s, the El Camino still sold every bit as well as the Ranchero had during its final five years, with annual tallies remaining above 20,000 until 1986. But GM planners, too, recognized reality, only this time the handwriting on the wall differed from what Ford people had read nearly 10 years before. Two all-new trends had taken root during the 1980s, one involving the increasingly popular mini-van, the other centered around the then-emerging sport-utility breed, and both turned customers' attentions away from the half-car/half-truck hybrid. So it was that the El Camino trail reached its end early in 1988.

Though long gone from the production line, the El Camino remains popular today. Itcan still be commonly seen doing what it always did best, working and playing with the best of them.

Above
One of many dress-up options offered during the El Camino's long run, the Royal Knight package also included this hood treatment, which was very reminiscent of the more familiar hood found on Pontiac's Trans Am.

Far left
This heavily accessorized El Camino was one of 21,508 built for 1986. Production then fell to 13,743 in 1987 before the end of the road finally came early in 1988.

Sixties Sensations
All-New Trucks for an All-New Decade

Nice vans to have around the house . . . or business

Chevy-Vans & Sportvans

Both Chevy-Van and Sportvan offer two lengths, two wheelbases, two capacities and Six or V8 power. The ½-ton models offer up to 209 cubic feet of payload space on a 90-inch wheelbase. The 256-cubic-foot body, mounted on a 108-inch wheelbase, can be ordered with either ½- or ¾-ton

chassis components. All models utilize durable tapered leaf springs. And all can be outfitted with several interior arrangements. Whichever model you choose Chevrolet's stay-tight integral body-frame construction takes all the punishment you can dish out . . . on the job or around the house.

Chevy-Van

Above
The popular Chevy van was introduced in December 1963 and revamped in 1967. Standard power originally came from a four-cylinder, Chevy's first truck-line four-banger since 1928. Shown here is the 1969 model.

Left
Stepsides remained popular into the 1960s, but Fleetsides would overtake them by the end of the decade.

The Fabulous 1950s ended just as they had begun, with Chevrolet still building America's best-selling truck. Twenty years and counting and the string remained strong. Make that stronger. Just as 1950 was a big year for the longtime leader, so too was 1960. While total truck market production in 1960 experienced a 5 percent growth compared to 1959's tally, Chevrolet's 1960 increase was a whopping 21 percent. Calendar-year production was nearly 395,000, the second highest total since Chevrolet's record-setting performance of 10 years earlier. The decade may have been new but the news wasn't. But before you digest that news, let's take a moment to dissect the various ways it was reported.

Claiming "best-selling" honors long has been a big deal to the advertising barkers in both the car and truck markets. And Detroit's two low-priced rivals, Chevrolet and Ford, have been doing all the barking on both sides of that fence for more than 75 years now. Various close calls have come over those years; a couple so close they never were really resolved, even after further review.

Take 1957's automobile sales race. Like the Bush-Gore presidential tug-of-war of 2000, they're probably still down there somewhere in the bowels of beancounter hell rechecking this one. College football's Bowl Championship Series panel couldn't have done it any better. When the tire smoke cleared after one of Detroit's greatest years ever, both Chevrolet and Ford claimed top honors for 1957. Who cheated? Well, maybe Ford a little; but Chevy made some accounting adjustments too. Dearborn execs had been dedicated to unseating Chevrolet atop the industry rankings for far too long; no way were they going to let the fact that their 1957 model year actually ran for 13 months get in the way of a well-earned honor. When that extended period ended late in November, they claimed they'd built 1,674,488 1957 cars. Chevrolet's 1957 model run, which typically had begun in the fall of the previous year and then lasted 12 months, produced a final count of 1,515,177 coupes, sedans, station wagons and the rest. With all precincts in, Ford officials couldn't help but look across town for a concession speech.

119

Meanwhile, their counterparts at Chevrolet were doing the same, and not because they were expecting a recount. Whether a 1957 Ford was sold in October 1956 or November 1957, it still counted the same, even if it was purchased in Palm Beach County, Florida. Discounting that extra month wouldn't have made up the difference anyway, and there was not one chad—hanging, dimpled, or otherwise—to be found anywhere.

stats when all you need to know is "just the facts?" Fact is, Chevrolet trucks were number one for 30 years. No one can argue that. Not Democrats or Republicans. Not cats or dogs. And certainly not Ford or Dodge.

Oversimplification also comes into play within these pages concerning the way calendar-year numbers were determined over the years. Before World War II, officially published annual production tallies based their numbers on new registrations for the year in question. Registration counts always ran well short of actual calendar-year production, a more realistic reflection that came into vogue (at least in Chevrolet terms) in 1936. From a truth-in-reporting perspective, model-year scores should be the only ones that count, but these statistics (along with yearly individual model breakdown numbers) never gained serious consideration in the truck field until three or four decades ago. Nowadays we seemingly count every bean, no matter how trivial.

Making for even more mind-numbing numbers is the confusing fact that annual market segment percentages have been published over the years based on all the various counts: calendar-year registrations, calendar-year sales or production figures, and model-year sales or production totals. Thus, you'll often see different percentages listed for the various postwar highs established by Chevrolet in the market-share category during the 1950s and 1960s. Suffice it to say that Chevy always hogged the biggest slice.

Whatever the exact percentage was, Chevrolet's piece of the commercial-vehicle pie in 1960 was as heaping a helping as anyone around Detroit had seen since Chevy's big bite in 1950. And after dipping slightly in 1961, the company's share of the truck market continued going up each succeeding year until 1966"".

Chevrolet didn't top its 1950 market-share number during the 1960s but did establish various production records. Nineteen-sixty-two's calendar-year score (396,658) was the highest dating back to 1950. That 12-year-old record then was left behind in 1963 after production surpassed 400,000 for the first time since 1951. In turn, 1963's new all-time high (483,119) lasted only 12 months, as Chevy trucks soared past the 500,000 mark for the first time in 1964—this even after a month-long United Auto Workers' strike had halted production of an estimated 50,000 units that year.

Although the cab roof was lowered in 1960, interior room did not shrink, thanks to a lowered floor—no more step up into the passenger compartment. Notice that knee-threatening "dogleg" at the bottom corner of the wraparound windshield.

What Chevy's paper-pushers did was reshuffle the stack. They concluded that their company's calendar-year production—cars built between January and December 1957—was 1,522,536, compared to Ford's comparable calendar-year total of 1,522,406. Bingo, Chevrolet was once more the big winner, if only by a piddling 130 Bel Airs, Corvettes, and Nomads.

If the game doesn't end in your favor, just find another scorekeeper, or calculate by calendar-year, model-year—whatever works. If that didn't work out in your favor, there was even more ambiguity to be found in sales figures and production figures, two annual measurements that never equate either. In this epic tome you'll see "sales" and "production" used interchangeably when describing the annual performance of Chevrolet's truck assembly lines. While not technically correct, this oversimplification occurs out of poetic license—why fret about specific

Right
All-new styling on a redesigned chassis made big news on the 1960 truck market. Notice the 1960 El Camino in the background.

officials there were 4,751,127 Chevy trucks of all ages working in 1965. On the road, on the job, wherever.

Chevrolet's soaring successes of the 1960s were the results of both the products' ever-refining merits and the growing momentum of the truck market in general. When Chevy first tested the commercial-car waters in 1918, the company ended up selling one truck for every 104 automobiles that year. By 1963 the ratio had reached one for every six, and this trend at the time was increasing market-wide, too. Up nearly 20 percent compared to 1962—when annual truck sales surpassed 1 million for the first time—1963's truck total represented 13.9 percent of that year's entire vehicle market, another record. Three additional new record years

Wait till you feel what torsion springs have done for truck handling

"You don't have to be a truck driver to drive this one." . . . "Really hangs on the road, doesn't fishtail or whip around." . . . "Like driving a car with power steering." . . . "You don't get the swerve and sway you get on most trucks." . . . "My wife says I'm easier to get along with since I've been driving this truck."

Those are some of the things the drivers are saying—the men who live in trucks all day long and know a new kind of handling ease when they feel it. They're sold.

Owners are sold, too. They like their drivers happy. They also like the way Chevy's Torsion-Spring Ride lets them work faster, get in more trips a day. Quote: "I can average a load a day

1960 CHEVROLET

Chevrolet plants built 55,324 trucks in April 1964 alone—you guessed it, another new record. The 600,000 barrier was shattered in 1965, and a fourth consecutive record year ended with yet another all-time high (621,417) in 1966.

If those numbers appear huge to you, they should. Thirty percent of all Chevrolet trucks built during its 48-year history left the firm's factories during the period from 1960 to 1966. The company sold its 7 millionth truck in 1959. The 8 millionth followed in 1962, the 9 millionth in 1964, and the 10 millionth in 1966. Those pickups, vans, and dump trucks not only were rolling off assembly lines at ever-growing rates, they were also sticking around. According to Chevrolet

followed in this case, too. Was it any wonder, then, that the press denoted 1965 as "The Year of the Truck"?

Nineteen-sixty-five was also "The Year of General Motors" as Detroit's corporate giant became the first American business venture of any kind to earn $2 billion or more in a year. GM's sales for 1965 were 20 percent higher than 1964's. Its market share was 52.1 percent in 1964, and 53.1 percent in 1965.

Runaway truck sales obviously played a role in reaping that windfall, and that rise in turn was the product of an unprecedented jump in pickup popularity. Along with Ford and Dodge, GM's Chevrolet/GMC truck tandem claimed 84 percent of 1965's sales. Of course, save for the big-rig boys, by then International and Kaiser-Jeep were the only other real competitors left. That's not the point, though. Chevrolet and Ford rose so

Deluxe treatments abound on this 1961 Apache, a situation more commonly seen during the 1960s as Chevrolet's light trucks began taking on more class and style.

123

luxury items totaled about 65,000 in 1961. Five years later that figure had more than tripled. More and more boat trailers were hitching rides too by the mid-1960s. And, although some cars and station wagons could handle smaller vessels and campers, the truly smart choice in towing was of course the light truck.

Transforming pickups into playthings supplied much of the momentum for the evolution of the all-purpose, market-dominating utility vehicle we have today. While Chevrolet's Cameo Carrier undoubtedly represented Detroit's first subtle turn in this direction, it was the rapidly mobilizing vacationing crowd of the 1960s who really got things rolling. Reportedly two out of three pickups then on the road were doing double-duty as work trucks during the week and recreational vehicles on the weekends. The civilization of the four-wheel-drive vehicle would soon be influencing evolution, too, but that's another story for another chapter.

It was the camping and boating craze more than any other fad, frenzy, or factor that helped feed the ever-growing truck market of the 1960s. At the same time the rise of the recreational vehicle also inspired a second trend that itself would soon grow into a force to be reckoned with. Pulling boats and towing trailers required primo power, and nothing put out power better than a V-8.

Installing an optional V-8 was always recommended, if not required, whenever a customer ordered a vehicle with towing in mind in the 1960s. Thus, as camping and boating grew in popularity, so too did the V-8 pickup. When Chevrolet announced a more powerful 327-ci V-8 option for its 1965 three-quarter- and one-ton models, witnesses knowingly nodded their heads. According to *Automotive News*, Chevy's truck-line 327 was created "to meet the needs of the booming recreational vehicle market."

Chevrolet officials also coincidentally chose that year to announce a second new truck option, RPO Z81, the Camper Special package. Ford actually began 1965 with its own Camper Special deal; Chevy simply followed suit midyear. Offered for the three-quarter-ton C20 V-8 pickup, RPO Z81 beefed up the suspension with a thick front stabilizer bar, heavy-duty rear shocks, auxiliary rear springs, and oversized (7.50x16) tires. The option also included big West Coast side mirrors, a tinted windshield with two-speed wipers, a deluxe

far above the rest because they concentrated on pickups, and pickups were among the 1960s' hottest tickets. Big trucks gained a lot of ground in the 1960s, too, but nowhere near as much as their light-duty cousins.

One more major milestone was realized in 1965: light trucks (those with a 6,000-pound GVW rating or less) reached the 1 million mark in sales for the first time in history. From then on there was little doubt as to whether the pickup belonged in the transportation mainstream. It not only belonged, it soon would be making its own waves.

Various factors, all of them familiar, helped make the American pickup's eventual entry into polite society possible. As mentioned profusely here, improving comfort, convenience, and looks had been keys from the beginning. But two other variables, both intertwined, also emerged in the 1960s to soundly certify the light truck's admission into the American mainstream.

By 1960 Average Joe, his family, and friends were finding themselves with more leisure time on their hands—as well as more disposable funds in their bank accounts—than ever before. What to do? Many middle-classmates began buying recreational toys: travel trailers, truck campers and camping trailers. Sales of these three

The Numbers Game

It was only logical that Chevrolet's earliest trucks relied on the same designations as their passenger-car counterparts. After all, the Model 490 truck was simply a Model 490 automobile with the excess bodywork traded for rudimentary cabs and cargo boxes supplied by outside contractors. While various alphabetized model codes were applied directly to Chevy trucks to follow, the model lines' main monikers continued to come from the car side of the assembly line.

Individuality and continuity finally entered the equation after the end of World War II. First came an all-new code system based on load capacity that would stay in place up through the 1950s. The basic half-ton pickup was a 3100-series model, the 3600 series featured three-quarter-ton trucks, and so on. One-ton pickups were in the 3800 series.

Half-ton (3100) and three-quarter-ton (3600) series numbers appeared as badges on Advance-Design hoods in 1949. Adjustments to this system included the addition of a 3200 series in 1955 to accommodate the new "long-box" light-truck. Compared to the base 1955 pickup that rolled on a 114-inch wheelbase, the model 3204 half-ton truck featured a lengthened bed on the 3600 three-quarter-ton's longer 123.25-inch chassis. A second new code, model 3124, also showed up in 1955 to mark the arrival of the glorious Cameo Carrier.

That same 3100/3200/3600/3800 system carried over for Chevy pickups (light- and medium-duty) into 1958, but each weight class now had a real model name. Light-duty trucks wore "Apache" emblems, medium-duties were named "Viking," and the heavies received "Spartan" badges. Weight-class numbers on the badges were also reduced to the first two digits used in the previous classification. In the light-duty line, a standard half-ton wore a "31" badge, the long-box half-ton "32," and so on. Some additional bright script—added to announce the arrival of the Fleetside model—appeared mid-year at the tail of the new slab-sided cargo box.

In a valiant effort to simplify things, Chevrolet officials designed a totally different system for the new 1960 Chevy truck. A one-letter code now identified the individual types: "C" denoted the conventional truck, "K" represented the four-wheel-drives, "P" meant forward-control, "L" stood for low cab forward, "S" signified school bus, and "M" was reserved for the big tandem-axles. A two-digit number after the letter clued people in to the weight classification: "10" was a half-ton, "20" a three-quarter-ton, "30" a one-ton, and "40" a one-and-a-half-ton. This system became more involved on paper with extra numbers to signify the body style and wheelbase, but the designation for a typical half-ton Chevy pickup in 1960 was a "C10."

Although various model monikers (Cheyenne, Silverado) have surfaced over the years, the basic "C/K" system has remained in place to this day, and the only real change involved an evolution of the numbers that followed those letters. C/K pickups today are labeled 1500 (half-ton), 2500 (three-quarter-ton), or 3500 (one-ton). An uncomplicated code system has been a plus in recent years considering how many model variations now exist in the C/K line. It's almost a matter of not being able to tell the players apart without a scorecard, but that's what numbers are for, right?

The "3100" series badge first appeared on Chevy pickup hoods in 1949. It briefly disappeared, then returned in 1953. This is the 1954 rendition.

A new series, the 3200 "long-box" half-ton with its extended wheelbase, appeared in 1955. Shown here is the badge on a 1957 long-box.

The model series number dropped the last two digits on Chevy truck badges beginning in 1958, the same year model names were introduced. Light trucks were Apaches, medium-duty models were Vikings, and heavy-duty trucks were Spartans. This is a 1959 Apache Fleetside fender.

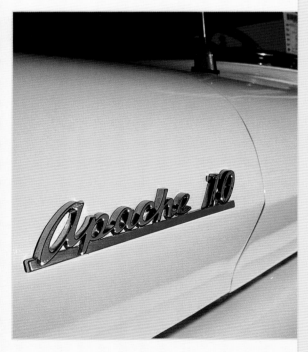

The 31, 32, etc. model-series progression was switched to 10, 20, 30 in 1960. Half-tons were C10 models, although only the digits initially showed up on badges. Shown here is a 1961 Apache pickup.

heater/defroster, a radio, and dual visors. Various deluxe exterior dress-up was thrown in, too. All the customer had to do was slip in the camper of his choice and go wherever he wanted, confident that he had bought the right truck for the job—make that adventure—at hand.

As for the V-8 aspect of Chevy pickup progress in the 1960s, this supreme power source was of course nothing new then. But, although Chevrolet and V-8s had been together since 1955, most buyers in the 1950s still felt the old, reliable Stovebolt six was good enough for them. Even in 1960, six-cylinder models made up 86 percent of Chevy truck production—not that the optional 283 Trademaster V-8 was a bad buy in those days. Economy wasn't that much of an issue then, considering that gasoline was still dirt-cheap, and the V-8's price tag—$92 throughout the early 1960s—didn't exactly represent an arm and a leg, either. (An arm, maybe, but certainly not a leg.) Apparently truck customers simply needed some time to warm up to V-8s. The recreational vehicle then stepped up to supply a little shove and bam; V-8-powered Chevy pickups were soon all the rage.

About 100,000 more V-8s were installed in 1964 than the previous year. The six-cylinder score had dropped to 78.6 percent by 1963; then it really started falling, all the way down to 55 percent the next year. Chevrolet built about 50,000 V-8 trucks in 1960. That figure soared to 250,000 in 1966 when the V-6–versus–V-8 bias slipped further to 60/40. The V-8s finally outsold six-cylinders for the first time in 1968.

Let's not forget the trucks that these V-8s went into. Although some historians have labeled the 1960–66 period as "the V-8 era," there was more going on then than muscle-flexing. Much more.

All-new styling was the most obvious improvement in 1960. Parked next to its brawny, purposeful-looking Task-Force predecessor, the 1960 Chevy C-10 (badging was new too) half-ton was so much sleeker in overall appearance. Company promotional paperwork called the new look one of "clean, functional lines." "More civilized" might' have been a fair description, too, as it impressed many as "car-like" to the greatest degree yet. Leading the way up front were those same jet engine nacelles that Claire MacKichan's styling team had incorporated into their 1959 passenger-car make-over.

Quad headlights, another trendy GM car-line touch that first shone brightly on Cadillac's Eldorado Brougham in 1957, simply carried over from the Task-Force trucks.

Though clearly quite "busy" by today's aesthetic standards, Chevy's new pickup nose did supposedly signify sleek and clean in 1960, if only by association. GM designers had become infatuated with aircraft during the late 1950s, and their work showed it big-time on both cars and trucks. The logic was simple: Jet fighters of the day were certainly sleek and slick, so mimicking their engine intakes on the front of a truck surely would impart similar impressions. Right? Okay, most critics today would consider that nose overdone, if not downright garish. But you have to take into account that tastes naturally change (especially over 40 years), and the styles popular in 1960 had yet to shake off the residue of the fabulously flashy 1950s. That high-flying look fit right in then, though not for long.

Just as the times were soon a-changin', so too apparently were tastes around Chevrolet's truck styling studio. Designers toned down frontal appearances in 1962, letting form better follow function in the best interests of the "less is more" ideal. Out went those intimidating, lost-in-the-Fifties quad headlights; in went equally functional, much simpler conventional duals. All that aircraft-inspired imagery at the hood's leading edge was also deleted, leaving the turn signals to work alone in far less cluttered surroundings.

Save for different trim, restyled grilles and headlight housings, and relocated badges, the only other exterior change worth noting came in 1964 when a trendy, lightly-curved windshield replaced the big wraparound glass used from 1960 to 1963. Another GM-favored fad from the 1950s, the wraparound windshield introduced along with the "60 Chevy pickup, bent even further around the cab corners than its 1959 counterpart. The result was an even more pronounced "dog-leg" in the door—yet another design aspect familiar to car owners of the 1950s, many of whom still have the scars on their knees to prove it. Getting out of a pickup cab in 1964 no longer meant occasionally banging up a knee, because that new windshield did away with that dog-leg.

With the last 1950s leftover left behind, those "clean, functional lines" were allowed to truly shine

after 1964, just as they had from the beginning behind that bold facade. Discounting the nose, the sharp-edged new-for-1960 pickup body indeed was crisply simple and straightforward, with only a full-length waistline crease interrupting the view. Inspiration for adding that crease undoubtedly came from the various slings and arrows hurled at Ford's first Styleside truck of 1957, a rounded-corner, boxy machine that many curbside critics called "a refrigerator on wheels."

Helping set the new Chevy apart further from its 1950s-style rival (which Ford carried over into 1960) was the 1960s-style nature of those functional lines. Longer, lower, and wider had become the big deal in automotive design in 1957 after Virgil Exner's sleek, stunning Chryslers made the scene. GM's award-winning "Wide-Track" Pontiac then appeared in 1959 to "certify" those standards for the decade to come. In 1960 Chevrolet designers simply applied similar thinking to their trucks. Wheelbase (for the standard C10) was stretched an inch to 115, resulting in a corresponding increase in overall length from 185.7 inches in 1959 to 186.75—not exactly a noticeable jump. But the new body appeared to the eye to be much longer and wider than 1959's, thanks to a flatter roofline and a radically lowered stance. Overall height dropped seven inches in 1960, due apparently to that chopped roof. Looks though were a little deceiving.

Even with its shortened roofline, the cab's interior dimensions curiously expanded on all fronts. This represented a potential pain in the knee, yes, but that big Panoramic windshield helped boost total glass area, and thus visibility, considerably. The seat was five inches wider, making for 5.1 inches more shoulder room and 5.8 extra inches for the hips. And, seemingly surprisingly, headroom too went up by 1.3 inches. A shorter cab with more headroom? How was that possible?

Chevrolet's truck designers had again looked over the shoulders of their car-line counterparts for a little help violating physical laws. The key to the 1960 pickup's shortened stance was its new drop-center, X-member frame. If this foundation appeared familiar to Chevy fans it should have—a similar design had been rolled out as a base for 1958 passenger-cars.

Task-Force pickups in 1959 sat up high on a ladder-type frame that ran true and straight in profile from nose to

Far left
Various trim changes and new grilles continued setting Chevy pickups apart in 1964, 1965, and 1966. The most radical change involved the switch from the wraparound windshield to mildly curved front glass in 1964. Shown here is a 1965 C10 pickup.

Far left inset
By 1965 the Chevy pickup interior was as clean, classy, and convenient as it had ever been. The dashboard layout had debuted the year before.

tail. The new frame in 1960 also was a ladder-type in that it consisted of parallel (in plan view) rails tied together by lateral cross-members. But instead of straight (from a profile perspective) rails, the 1960 frame incorporated dropped side channels that ran down low between the front and rear wheels. Dropping the frame's center section made for a lower cab floor that was in turn flatter—being closer to the ground, it no longer needed those steps found inside the doors of Task-Force trucks, a fact greatly appreciated by skirt-wearing women passengers. Skirt-watching male drivers no longer got an occasional "show" after 1960.

What they did get was a roomier cab on a stronger frame that hugged the road better than ever. The lowered floor meant the cab roof could be lowered too without reducing headroom. Meanwhile, that big, heavy X-member in the middle, working in concert with boxed frame rail sections at the front and rear wheel areas, made for a much more torsionally rigid foundation. Finally, the end result of the dropped frame and shorter cab was a lower center of gravity. And, as we all know, lowering a vehicle's center of gravity immediately improves both ride and handling.

Additional improvement in these departments also came by way of revised suspension setups front and rear. In back, coil springs and long control arms with a lateral stabilizer bar replaced the more conventional parallel leaves used in 1959. Coils cushion road shocks more effectively than leaf springs, which tend to transmit bumps directly to the frame. Dirt and moisture also get trapped between those leaves, resulting in binding, creaking operation as corrosion takes over. Unless vastly overloaded, a garden-variety coil spring can't bind up, and rust is of no concern, at least not during the typical lifetime of a typical truck.

Far more noteworthy was the 1960 Chevy's new front suspension, which traded the traditional (and obsolete) I-beam axle and parallel leaves for a car-style independent arrangement featuring upper and lower A-arms. Yet another concession to the civilization of the American pickup, independent front suspension (IFS) also improved ride by minimizing road shocks and smoothing out bumps. Nineteen-fifty-nine's solid front axle suspended by leaf springs sent those jars and jumps directly to the seat of the driver's pants. Stability was also compromised, as whenever one front wheel rode up over a bump, so too did that corner of the truck. The IFS

layout allowed each front wheel to absorb shocks separately, and suspension travel translated far less into vertical frame movements.

Independent front suspension represented another major milestone for the Chevrolet pickup. Ford didn't drop its old, clunky solid front axle until 1965, and even then it was Dearborn's compromising Twin I-Beam suspension that showed up amidst loads of hype and hoopla. It was 1997 before a modern short-arm/long-arm (SLA) independent front suspension debuted beneath Ford trucks. International Harvester introduced an IFS truck chassis in 1961; Dodge pickups finally joined the fraternity in 1972.

Chevrolet's ground-breaking IFS construction also incorporated additional cutting-edge technology. Modern ball-joints replaced those antiquated kingpins to greatly reduce steering effort. And, like International's fad-following independent front suspension of 1961, Chevy's 1960 design used torsion bars in place of the coil springs much more commonly found in SLA layouts. Packard pioneered the postwar automotive adaptation of torsion-bar suspension (for both front and rear wheels) back in 1955. Front torsion bars became a Chrysler chassis feature in 1957 for its cars only. Torsion bars reportedly insured an even softer ride than coil springs.

Chevrolet's chassis redesign resulted in a pickup that didn't just look a little like a car. A 1960 advertisement recited a list of testimonials to the new suspension's merits: "You don't have to be a truck driver to drive this.'" "Like driving a car with power steering." "You don't get the swerve and sway you get on most trucks." "My wife says I'm easier to get along with since I've been driving this truck."

"A new standard in truck performance" was Chevrolet's own description of its new IFS chassis. "Handling characteristics are greatly improved; there's less roll and sway, less shimmy and wheel fight," added brochures. "And because objectionable road shocks are cushioned out, there's far less damage to truck, cargo and tires. Longer truck life, tire life, lower maintenance expense and reduced driver fatigue result. You get more work done, more economically, than ever before."

Maybe so, but Chevrolet engineers apparently opted for lower standards in 1963. Conventional coils replaced the torsion bars that year, basically because the latter design mandated the use of an extra-heavy-duty X-member frame. Switching to conventional coils meant that the X-member bracing could be deleted, a move that in turn did away with a lot of unwanted weight. Another change came in back, as the rear coils were upgraded to two-stage progressive units. These variable-rate coil springs reportedly kept the ride nice when the truck was empty, then went to work more firmly once pounds started piling on. Also new for 1963 was a Delcotron alternator in place of the generator used previously on all engines.

The really big news for 1963 involved the arrival of two new engines to go along with those alternators. Chevy's venerable Stovebolt six, in business since 1929, was finally replaced as the base power source for the company's two-wheel-drive pickups. (K-series 4x4s still used the old engine.) The 1963 C10's base engine was a lighter, more compact, short-stroke 230-ci six-cylinder created using the thinwall casting technique that had become all the rage around Detroit in the early-1960s. An optional 292-ci six replaced the 261-cube six offered in 1962. Both new sixes featured lightweight rocker arms modeled from the stamped-steel individual rockers used by Chevy's high-winding small-block V-8. At the bottom end was a tough crankshaft now held in place by seven main bearings to insure the reciprocating assembly would continue reciprocating under considerable stress for many, many miles.

Along with being more durable and less massive, the new High-Torque six-cylinder family also produced a few extra ponies compared to its 1962 predecessors. The 230 six's maximum output was 140 horses at 4,400 rpm in 1963, compared to the 235 Trademaster's 135 at 4,000. The 261 Trademaster made 150 horsepower at 4,000 revs, the 292 High-Torque six developed 165 at 3,800 turns.

A third new High-Torque engine, a 90-horse 153-ci four-cylinder, was also introduced in 1963 for Chevrolet's lightest P-series Step Vans. The division's first truck-line four-banger since 1928, this little economizer was actually created to help a new utility model better meet the challenges posed by Ford's Econoline vans.

Chevrolet's air-cooled Corvair 95 vans, introduced in 1961, couldn't quite keep up with sales- or performance with Dearborn's more conventional cracker boxes on wheels. Thus, they were joined in December 1963 by GM's first Chevy Van, a mover and shaker in the commercial-vehicle market that had already become a legend well before it was immortalized in song by Sammy Johns in 1975. This G-model van continued in the

forward-control tradition but housed its standard water-cooled four-cylinder up front between the seats, meaning it didn't have the hump in the floor ""that the Corvair 95 vans and pickups required in the back to house that pancake six-cylinder. The Chevy Van's full-length flat cargo floor allowed its owner to lay anything (or anyone) back behind those seats. Six-cylinder power was optional.

Optional pickup power was enhanced in 1966 when the aforementioned 327-ci small-block, limited the prior year to the larger C20 and C30 trucks, was made available for C10 half-tons. Chevrolet's first factory-installed in-dash air conditioner was also introduced for trucks in 1965. Before then, only dealer-installed add-on air conditioning had been available inside a Chevy pickup cab.

Enhanced safety also joined the new features collection in 1966 thanks to stiffer federal mandates. Stricter safety regulations passed down from Washington led to standard seatbelts, two-speed windshield wiper/washers, an outside mirror, and backup lights. Standard prices for 1966 increased accordingly, but not enough to sway buyers into shopping somewhere else.

Nearly 50 years after they first put rubber to the road, Chevy trucks were still Detroit's best buy in the cargo-hauling field, but Ford was not far behind. Chevrolet's record-setting sales performance of 1966 represented a pinnacle, a peak that naturally had to have a downside. And that slippery slide waited ahead just around the bend.

The C10's optional 283-ci V-8 produced 175 horsepower in 1965. An optional 327 small-block was also available for heavier pickups that year.

Putting The Driver First

Corvair 95 Pickups
1961–1964

Above
While Ford's record-setting Falcon relied on a conventional chassis with the engine in front and a live axle in the rear, Chevrolet engineers chose a much more innovative route for its compact response. The Corvair made headlines in 1960 with its rear-mounted air-cooled engine and four-wheel independent suspension.

Left
Chevrolet introduced its compact Corvair in 1960 then rolled out its Corvair 95 truck line in 1961. The family resemblance is apparent on these two 1964 models.

Introduced in the fall of 1959, both Ford's Falcon and Chevrolet's Corvair hit the ground running, with Dearborn's popular compact shattering Detroit's first-year sales record for an all-new model. Clearly America now was ready for small cars, although apparently it had not been just a few years before. Compacts were by no means new in this country when the rear-engined Corvair and more conventional Falcon debuted, but the concept never could quite catch the fancy of American car buyers before the 1960s.

Independents Crosley, Kaiser, Nash, and Hudson all had tried to introduce our ancestors to downsizing a decade or two before, with baseball-team-owning, home-appliance-king Powel Crosley's first efforts dating all the way back to the late-1930s. Imported mini-machines too began infiltrating the U.S. market after World War II, but they represented more of a nuisance than a threat to Detroit—for the time being. Although fat-and-happy American auto makers would later receive their comeuppance courtesy of compacts built in Japan, basically no one in 1960 could have predicted just how big a role small cars—or small trucks for that matter—would end up playing in the 1970s and 1980s.

Compact commercial vehicles have been around in the States even longer than their automotive counterparts. Among the first was American Austin's pint-sized pickup, first built in Butler, Pennsylvania, in 1929. Weighing barely half a ton, this truly small hauler could be hauled itself by most of today's pickups. Anyone now who actually remembers these little trucks probably better recognizes the name used after 1936: American Bantam. American Bantam pickups were marketed through 1941.

Right
Chevrolet's pancake six was mated to a transaxle in what promotional people called a "Unipack Power Team." You are looking at the Unipack's tail—the engine was mounted to the rear of the transaxle.

Below
The Corvair's air-cooled opposed six-cylinder was named "Turbo-Air." It displaced 145 cubic inches and was fed by twin carburetors.

The previous year, 1940, that irrepressible refrigerator magnate from Cincinnati had introduced his own commercial vehicle line based on the mini-cars he manufactured in Indiana. Powel Crosley's quarter-ton pickup was not much more than a Crosley automobile with a cargo box in place of the rear bodywork. And, like those diminutive Crosley cars, Crosley trucks never quite caught on, though they did survive into the early 1950s.

Undoubtedly the most qualified candidate for the role of "America's first compact pickup" came from Willys-Overland in 1957. The initial guiding force behind the lovable Jeep, Willys had already proven itself in both the lightweight utility and four-wheel-drive fields before the 1950s came along to reinforce the all-American belief that bigger had to be better. But even as Detroit's cars were growing ever larger, heavier, and more chrome-encrusted, the Kaiser-owned Willys

company in Toledo, Ohio, was exploring the possibility that less somehow could be more.

Willys' FC-150 wasn't simply a compact car with a miniscule cargo box tacked on in back. It was a true truck through and through, albeit a smaller truck than most Americans were accustomed to in 1957. Its wheelbase measured only 81 inches—a mere one inch longer than the tiny Crosley's hub-to-hub stretch—yet its cargo capacity ranked right up near that of many rival pickups. How was that possible?

Simple. The "FC" in the name stood for "forward-control," an arrangement that had been familiar to cabover big-rig drivers for years. Volkswagen was the first to offer Americans a forward-control pickup in the early 1950s. Willys then translated this German ideal into its FC-150, joined in 1957 by the longer, heavier FC-170.

The forward-control idea was simple. By putting the steering wheel ahead of the front wheels, the FC platform allowed the driver to sit farther forward relative to his place behind the wheels of typical pickups. All this relocation resulted in a smaller cab. You do the math: a smaller cab translated into more room on a shorter

frame for a longer bed. Even with its tidy wheelbase, Willys' FC-150 still featured a cargo box that measured a tad more than six feet from cab to tailgate.

That decent-sized bed and 5,000-pound gross vehicle weight meant the compact FC-150 could work nearly as hard as many conventional pickups. And thanks to that 81-inch wheelbase, turning radius was a scant 18-feet, easily the tightest of any truck then on the market. Reformed Kaiser-Jeep built the last FC-150 in 1965.

By then Detroit's prime movers had already done what they have always done best: copy another's idea and claim it for their own. In 1961 both Chevrolet and Ford had entered the compact forward-control field, although the two rivals traveled in slightly different circles. Ford's Econoline followed closer in the FC-150's tracks. Chevy's forward-control pickup, on the other hand, was more of a Volkswagen knock-off than a Willys redo.

Like the Econoline, Chevrolet's Corvair 95 trucks used unitized body/frame construction. But differences dominated from there. First and foremost was that counter-culture foundation. Unlike its competitor from Dearborn, the Corvair 95 featured an engine mounted VW-style in back. That engine too was air-cooled, another atypical (from a Yankee perspective) engineering trait obviously borrowed from Volkswagen and expectedly passed over from Chevrolet's compact car side of the fence.

Standard power for the first Corvair 95 truck was the same 80-horse 145-ci Turbo-Air pancake six-cylinder found behind backseats of 1961 Corvair Monzas. Standard transmission fare was a three-speed manual, with a four-speed stick and a "special Corvair 95" two-speed Powerglide automatic available at extra cost. Sandwiched between that pancake six and whatever transmission chosen was a transaxle final-drive unit coupled to either a clutch or torque converter, depending on the tranny choice. All together, this innovative engine/transaxle combo was called the "Unipack Power Package."

Chevrolet's factory paperwork called the Unipack package "the key element in the Corvair 95's totally new approach to truck design." "Combining engine, transmission and rear axle gearing in one unit," began the 1961 brochure, "it's small enough to fit between the rear

The Corvair 95 platform was of "forward-control" design, meaning the steering gear was mounted ahead of the front wheels. A raised rear-deck floor was required to clear the engine.

wheels and below a conventional-height load platform.' It's light enough in weight to combine rear installation with superior vehicle balance and weight distribution. And it's efficient enough to deliver performance that more than meets high American standards." Even with that air-cooled six perched way in back, the Corvair 95 pickup's 2,700-pound curb weight was equally distributed at both ends, an unprecedented achievement in light-truck construction.

Another aspect shared by Chevrolet and Ford's new light trucks in 1961 was their availability in both van and pickup forms. Actually, four different Corvair 95 models were introduced that year. At the top was the upscale, six-passenger Greenbriar window van. This classy van-about-town was marketed not as a truck but as a station wagon, even though it was simply a dressed-up version of the windowless Corvan, a Spartan, purely utilitarian vehicle clearly listed among Chevrolet trucks' ranks. Stripping off the Corvan's rear roof and upper cargo compartment walls created an unmistakable Corvair 95 truck, a true half-ton pickup offered in Loadside and Rampside forms.

As the name implied, the Corvair 95 Rampside featured a unique drop-down access ramp incorporated into the passenger's side of its cargo box just behind the cab. This wonderfully practical idea was made even more useful by the Corvair pickup's super-low main bed floor. Remember, there was no driveshaft running beneath Chevrolet's forward-control vehicle, a fact that allowed designers to lower that floor in back to a mere 14 inches off the ground. Working trigonometrically with the side-gate's 28-inch height, that low floor meant that a reasonably slight incline resulted when the ramp went down. And the resulting 47.5-inch-wide opening at the top of the ramp allowed almost any kind of cargo

CORVAIR 95
LOADSIDE
PICKUP

Nearly 28 inches deep, the Loadside's deep-well cargo area accommodates tall, bulky loads with ease. Weight is carried low and amidships for superior handling over the road.

Optional* level load floor extends versatility of deep cargo well, offers tailgate-level loading ease and protected stowage. Sectionalized construction permits partial use for special purposes.

Two Corvair 95 pickups were offered, the conventional Loadside and the clever Rampside with its passenger-side loading gate. Loadside models were only built for 1961 and 1962. The more popular Rampside rolled on into 1964.

easy entrance into the Rampside's box. Those clever designers even courteously wrapped a ribbed rubber mat over the gate's upper edge to prevent exterior paint damage whenever a lowered ramp made contact with grass, gravel, etc.

Calling the 1961 Rampside "the most important single new pickup truck development in 20 years," *Motor Trend*'s Bob Ames was obviously impressed with this intriguing vehicle's possibilities. "The importance of the side loading ramp might be overlooked by many persons," he wrote in *MT*'s July 1961 issue. "But to the small business man who must deliver heavy items such as furniture, it is exceptionally worthwhile. Ordinarily one man can load an item at the store where a dock is often available—but two men must be sent to get if off the truck. Not with a Rampside, however, and delivery charges can be virtually sliced in half. Overall the Corvair Rampside is not just another forward control pickup—it is a whole new concept in pickups."

If there was one downside to the idea, it involved the bed floor's multi-level layout. As amazingly compact as the Unipack powertrain was, a rise in the floor's rear section was still required to provide ample clearance. Some of the benefits gained by the loading ramp were

basically lost due to that cliff located behind the ramp's opening. Sure, that keg of Rolling Rock went up that ramp with ease. But if you were loading a weekend's supply of Latrobe's finest and had to move some of that suds to the rear, additional often-dreaded lifting was in order. Bummer.

Although a three-piece, plywood-and-angle-iron "Level Floor Option" was offered, it not only was a pain to place and remove, it of course also effectively negated the whole Rampside idea. In the end, a typical plank running down the tailgate of a typical half-ton pickup still proved equally effective—just as it had been before the Rampside came along.

Lost in the Rampside's shadow, the Loadside also could have been fitted with the Level Floor Option, as it too, of course, possessed the same inherent flaw in back. It also possessed the same cargo space, the same tailgate, the same bolt-down floor-panel/engine-cover, and the same engine access door below that tailgate. The only thing the two didn't share was the ramp.

Many buyers, however, didn't mind the split-level bed floor at all. That long lower section offered ample space for most of the lighter loads considered by the Corvair 95 owner. And with the bulk of its cargo space centered between the wheels, a balanced load basically was guaranteed every time, making the Loadside and Rampside a joy to drive even when cargo space was fully utilized. When empty, the two light trucks were as road worthy as some cars.

"The overall handling characteristics of the Rampside are superb, loaded or unloaded," continued Ames' raves. "This is something that is rarely true of a pickup. Since the weight is divided equally the truck handles as well as a Corvair sedan. Loads can be hauled in the center section where they maintain a low center of gravity and keep the weight equally divided between front and rear."

Of course, the Corvair 95 chassis featured an inherent handling advantage aside from that 50/50 weight balance. C'mon folks, Ralph Nader was wrong, dead wrong. Though there was a design problem early on involving the Corvair's rear suspension travel, that glitch was quickly fixed, leaving Chevrolet's compact a real road handler. And it just got better as the 1960s rocked and rolled on. Four-wheel independent suspension and a

Left
The Rampside was a popular pickup when introduced in 1961. This model is one of 14,893 built that year. Sales then lagged. Only 851 were built for 1964 before the breed was killed off.

Above inset
A small door below the tailgate allowed slight access to the Corvair 95 pickup's rear-mounted engine. But if a real problem did arise, the entire works could be exposed by unbolting the rear floor panel.

low center of gravity worked in concert with that neutral balance to wow most critics (save for Nader and his raiders) with the way this low-priced compact looked like a million bucks in the turns.

That independent arrangement (with heavier coils front and rear) carried over from the car side into the Corvair 95 ranks, although sturdier 14-inch wheels replaced the car's roller-skate-sized 13-inch rims at the corners. Other than the engine, that was about it as far as commonality was concerned between Corvair cars and trucks. As for the number in the name, that referred to the truck's wheelbase: 95 inches.

Those extra 14 inches (compared to the FC-150's wheelbase) allowed the agile Corvair 95 truck to turn a slightly wider circle than its forward-control forerunner from Willys. Nonetheless, no one could complain about the compact Chevy's 19.5-foot turning radius, a figure that still qualified as quite tight relative to typical pickups of the time.

More importantly, that extra length made even more room for cargo. With its forward-control cab taking up so little space up front, the pickup box in back was allowed to really stretch out. Bed floor length was about 8.5 feet, meaning 60 percent of overall length was devoted to cargo carrying—yet another unprecedented achievement. From a three-dimensional perspective that translated into 80 cubic feet of available cargo space, the most among 1961's pickup pack.

Also unprecedented was the Corvair truck's load capacity relative to its own weight. At only 2,700 pounds, the Rampside surely qualified as a compact. Its gross-vehicle-weight rating, however, was a decidedly un-compact 4,600 pounds, meaning the Corvair 95 pickup technically could carry 1,900 pounds.

"Never before has a truck design utilized space so efficiently, or been so completely engineered around the concept of maximum load-carrying ability," bragged Chevrolet brochures in 1961. "The list of new Corvair 95 design advantages goes on and on. They all add up to just one thing: Chevrolet's Corvair 95 offers a better, faster, easier, more economical way to do just about any light-duty job!"

Various advantages were also found up front. Thanks to its aft engine location, the Corvair 95 truck's cab was comfortably roomy, almost to the point of defying physical laws: it seemed bigger on the inside than it looked on the outside. Seating capacity was understandably superior in comparison to Ford's forward-control counterpart, as an Econoline driver and passenger had to share precious cab space with an inline six-cylinder powerplant planted between the seats. Chevrolet officials also liked to point out that putting the engine in the rear put all the noise and heat back there, too. Riding in a Corvair 95 truck represented a much more pleasant experience than a trip in an Econoline, which used archaic leaf springs and a solid I-beam axle up front.

Various other comparisons favored the Chevrolet as well. The Corvair 95 pickup's bed was nearly two feet longer than the Econoline's, and the former's payload rating surpassed the latter's by 250 pounds. It must be pointed out, though, that the Ford also weighed some 250 pounds less than the Chevy. The Econoline cost less, too: its base price in 1961 was $1,880, compared to the Loadside at $2,079 and the Rampside at $2,133. And though it displaced one less cubic inch, Ford's conventional, water-cooled 144-cube six-cylinder produced five more horses than Chevrolet's 80-horsepower air-cooled six. However, the Corvair 95 pickup was, by most accounts, better looking than the tall, gangly, snub-nosed Ford, this due to the Chevy's lower overall height (68.5 inches versus 78.5) and aesthetically superior proportions.

That last, totally subjective conclusion aside, the Econoline did in fact top the Corvair 95 in the one competition that counted most: sales. Econoline pickups outsold their Corvair rivals 14,893 to 13,262 in 1961. Chevrolet's fortunes quickly diminished from there. Rampside sales dipped down to 4,102 in 1962, 2,046 in 1963, and a mere 851 in 1964 before the model was mercifully discontinued, leaving only the aloof Greenbriar van to continue the Corvair 95 legacy for one more model run in 1965. The weakly received (2,475 sold in 1961, 369 in 1962) Loadside pickup had been cancelled after 1962, while the Corvan disappeared with the Rampside.

Econoline pickups, meanwhile, stuck around until 1967. But the last forward-control truck left standing was Dodge's A-100, introduced in 1964. From the beginning the A-100 was by far the most powerful of the three compacts. Then Chrysler engineers just had to go

Stepsides remained popular into the 1960s, but Fleetsides would overtake them by the end of the decade.

and drop in an optional V-8 in 1965. That boost notwithstanding, the Econoline continued outselling its only rival—by now a Dodge. The A-100 then found itself alone in the compact pickup field after 1967, probably for good reason. Declining demand left the forward-control A-100 fading into the sunset, with the end finally coming early in 1970.

Why was the Corvair 95 truck the first of the trio to fade away? Pricing undoubtedly played a major role. Not only did Chevrolet's forward-control pickup cost more than its direct competition; it also was more expensive than a typical Chevy half-ton of the day. A base-model Stepside pickup carried a $1,991 bottom line in 1961. And for less money, most contemporary conventional pickups surpassed the Rampside's maximum GVW rating by nearly 1,000 pounds. Finally, America probably wasn't quite ready for compact trucks in the early-1960s. A standard-sized half-ton still very much represented a real man's machine then.

Had the Rampside appeared a decade later, it just might have had a better chance at a longer life. In any case, the Corvair 95 pickup still was one cool, little truck—regardless of what Ralph Nader might have thought.

Far Left
The Greenbriar window-van continued on for one more year after the other Corvair 95 vehicles had retired.

Left
While the Corvan was intended only to haul cargo, the Greenbriar could seat the entire soccer team, making mom as happy as a clam.

Greenbriars were dressed up inside and out.

Still Crazy After All Those Years

Chevy Trucks Roll into the Seventies

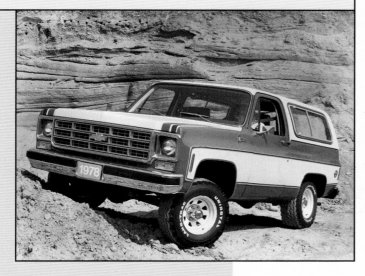

Above
Chevrolet helped kick the development of the modern SUV into passing gear in 1969 by introducing the Blazer, which originally came only as a 4x4 with a removable top. This is the 1978 version of the Blazer.

Left
As if the typical 1967 Chevy pickup wasn't good-looking enough on its own, there was also the Custom Sport Truck option. The CST package added extra trim outside and a sporty interior inside.

Even Cal Ripken, Jr., couldn't keep playing forever. The future Hall-of-Famer finally took a seat on the Baltimore Orioles bench in September 1998, ending an unprecedented streak of 2,632 straight games in the lineup—502 more than the indefatigable "Iron Horse" himself, New York Yankee Lou Gehrig, who played without a break from 1925 to 1939. Apparently most major-league baseball records are made to be broken. But Ripken's iron-willed achievement ranks right up with Cy Young's 511 wins and Ty Cobb's .367 career batting average on the summer game's short list of seemingly unreachable standards.

Was it any wonder, then, that GM chose Ripken to help promote the Chevrolet truck line? "Cal Ripken, Jr., personifies the same 'most dependable' and 'longest lasting' qualities we have been stressing in our full-size pickup truck advertising for years," said Silverado Brand Manager Kurt Ritter while announcing Chevy's next new pickup in January 1998. "He's a natural spokesperson to introduce Silverado."

Chevrolet's truck team members know a little about streaking, too—although their company's record-setting reign had ended about a quarter-century before Ripken came on board in August 1995. After 30 years in pursuit, Ford trucks had finally returned to the top seat in 1968 and were soon off on a long tear of their own. Perhaps Dearborn's promotional people are busy right now looking up Cal's number, as Ford's stretch stands on the verge of surpassing Chevrolet's long-running string.

Chevrolet pickups built between 1967 and 1972 remain the most popular by far among collectors today, partly because they were so popular then. Most critics 30-odd years ago called them the most attractive Chevy trucks yet. Notice the license plate on this 1968 half-ton—"Job Tamer" was the new ad slogan that year.

Like Ripken's uninterrupted 16-year run on the Orioles' infield, Chevy's unparalleled performance in the utility-vehicle field simply had to come to an end eventually and probably would have much earlier if not for a little luck here and there. Although they may have been stuck in second all during the 1940s and 1950s, Ford's tough truck-makers were by no means easily beaten bush-leaguers—they were capable of bouncing back to the top during almost any given year. Okay, so the first F-series pickup couldn't quite do the trick; the more modern F-100 narrowed the gap in 1954 before Chevrolet's Task-Force trucks appeared to rebuild the lead a year later. A revamped F-100 then edged right back into striking distance in 1957. And Ford actually sold more light trucks than Chevy in 1959, but superiority in the heavy-duty ranks that year kept the Bow-Tie

banner on top overall. Barely a percentage point or two worth of market share separated the two hard-fighting rivals in 1961.

The 1960s' unparalleled surge in pickup popularity apparently benefited the challenger slightly more than the champ. By 1966 Ford was on a real roll and undoubtedly would have severed Chevy's string the following year had a United Auto Workers' Union strike not idled Blue-Oval plants for two months. Nineteen-sixty-eight's calendar-year count then put Dearborn back in front of the truck race for the first time since 1937. All good things indeed must come to an end.

That's not to say, however, that Chevy pickups were no longer great trucks after 1966. On the contrary, they were the greatest yet, and the most popular, too. Watching Ford rise back up to number one wasn't all

CST trucks were fitted with appropriate door badges. The stylish wheel covers were extras.

that painful for Chevrolet officials, considering they also saw their truck division reach new production highs in 1968 and 1969. GM's own labor woes cut into 1970's numbers, then more company records followed in 1971 and 1972. During that latter year Chevy sold more than 500,000 half-tons alone for the first time in history, reflecting a market trend toward increased pickup sales. According to Department of Commerce findings, about 63 percent of the working truck population in 1972 consisted of pickups.

Dearborn, meanwhile, was establishing all-time industry highs during those years as both rivals benefited mightily from a bull market the likes of which Detroit-watchers had never seen before. Total truck sales for 1970 more than doubled 1960's score, and the market surpassed 2 million for the first time ever in 1971. In 1972 the truck's piece of the automotive industry pie reached 20 percent for the first time. Truck sales broke the 3 million barrier in 1973 and the 4 million mark in 1978. Nineteen-seventy-eight's market share was 27.9 percent, a record that would stand until 1984.

Ford's 1972 truck sales record remained in the books for only one year, as Chevrolet jumped back up into the top slot in 1973 with another new body, this one sticking around in the same basic form (treated to a couple modernizing makeovers) for 15 years. Chevy and Ford each built more than 1 million trucks for the first time in 1973, meaning there was ample success to spread around regardless of which company was officially number one and which was number two.

Chevrolet's 1967-1972 models stand out in truck collectors' minds today for various reasons, not the least of which involves sheer numbers. These vehicles are so popular now because they were so popular then. Devoted fans have no problems finding decent survivors, and putting one back into tip-top original condition is equally easy both because parts remain plentiful and aftermarket suppliers have stepped up to help to a degree unmatched in the vintage pickup restoration business. This country's biggest, busiest light-truck restoration specialists focus not on Ford's first F-100s, nor any of the record-setting F-150s to follow. Chevrolet's own highly popular Task-Force models don't even draw as much attention as do the Bow-Tie-wearing pickups built between 1967 and

1972. Present-day owners are still crazy for them after all these years.

But don't think for a minute that these trucks remain hot tickets nearly 40 years down the road primarily due to their availability. As they did in the early 1970s, today's innocent, hopefully objective bystanders and biased, undoubtedly unabashed loyalists alike continue touting the 1967-72 pickups as the most attractive Chevy trucks built up to that point. Ad copy in 1967 wasn't just whistlin' Dixie when it claimed that that year's new

models featured "the most significant cab and sheetmetal styling change in Chevrolet history." Impressions were crisp, clean, and classy, and the Fleetside's cab and bed were more fully integrated than ever before.

The truck's appeal went much deeper than sheet metal. That significant cab was moved down even closer to the earth in 1967, a modification that both enhanced long, low lines and made it easier for occupants to exit and enter. A lowered stance also dropped the truck's center of gravity, which aided both ride and handling—

Far left
Bright pedal trim, a special horn button, lush carpeting, and "bucket" seats were included in the CST deal in 1967.

Above
Few changes were made to the 1968 Chevy truck, which remained as popular as its redesigned 1967 forerunner. Tougher safety regulations led to the installation of body side marker lights at both ends in 1968.

147

Above
The base V-8 in 1968 was this 307-ci small-block, rated at 200 horsepower. The 327 V-8 was optional. Other options on this 1968 C10 Custom included power steering, power brakes, and the Powerglide automatic transmission.

yet another example of concessions made to attract a kinder, gentler truck buyer. Like Ford, Chevrolet was selling so many trucks by the 1970s because those vehicles could both handle a dirty job and fit into polite society with near equal ease. They not only looked great on the outside, they also felt right from behind the wheel—so much so that for the first time it became possible to compare pickups with cars without having to squint your eyes to make the connection.

"Meet the world's toughest 2-door," announced 1967 advertisements for the new Chevy pickup, which, in some imaginations, might have passed for a traditional two-door coupe. Chevrolet's latest new-and-improved trucks represented the biggest breakthrough yet on the

road toward the modern, multi-tasking, everyday-operating utility vehicle we all know, many love, and half of us own today. Lessons learned from previous efforts to mate car with truck paid off in what advertising hype called "a brand new breed for 1967."

The 1967 Chevrolet, continued that ad, "was built for hard work, certainly; but, beyond that, it provides more style, comfort and convenience than trucks have before. We'll go so far as to say that it looks as good and rides as smooth as many cars. And is just about as comfortable inside."

Basically the same easier-on-the-seat-of-the-pants, easier-on-the-eyes Chevy truck carried on up through 1972 with few major changes. A recontoured leading edge for the hood came along in 1968, and grilles were restyled a couple times, perhaps most dramatically with the 1971 model, whose sporty egg-crate design mimicked the car line much as the first Task Force truck had back in 1955. But, while basic looks remained constant, there was still some noticeable stylin' and profilin' goin' on.

Truly fresh, definitely flashy trim treatments began to flourish in 1967. Chevrolet's latest dress-up deal, the Custom Sport Truck option, debuted that year to prove that promotional people again weren't blowing smoke when they referred to the revamped '67 model as "a new concept in personalized pickups." Previous Custom Cab renditions paled in comparison to the CST package, which was only offered on the fashionable Fleetside. Like its Custom counterparts, the CST featured a chrome front bumper, brighter trim here and there, and upscale interior appointments. Custom Sport Trucks received even more exterior dress-up (appropriate "CST" badges on the doors, silver anodized grille background, etc.), but

Chevrolet CAMPERS

When the name of the game is outdoor fun... look to the name, Chevrolet

All the qualities that make Chevrolet pickups shine on the job, make them outstanding recreational vehicles, too. In addition, an almost endless list of accessories is available to make any camp-out a fun-in. The list includes everything from stabilizer bars to air conditioning. Included among the many models is the

Series 20 Longhorn

Chevrolet Longhorn. It's the only pickup built that is designed especially for camping. Available in either ¾- or 1-ton sizes; it offers a longer wheelbase for better weight distribution and handling ease. For those who prefer self-contained units, Sportvans and Step-Vans can be easily converted into family-styled motor homes.

4-WHEEL DRIVE models

Designed to take over where roads leave off

Road or no road, very few areas are off limits with a 4 x 4 chassis. They're available with 6½- and 8-ft. pickup bodies, Suburban bodies and as chassis-cab units. These low-profile models provide high capacity front axles plus tapered leaf

springs for an easy ride over the roughest of terrains. Transfer case is attached to the transmission through an adapter which permits a low vehicle height without sacrificing ground clearance. Try one ... they'll go anywhere.

the real treat came inside. Full carpeting (even over the gas tank at the cab's back wall) and a Chevy truck first, bucket seats, represented the main attractions. A center armrest served double-duty as a storage console, and it also flipped up to create a third-passenger seat. A special horn button, bright pedal trim, and chrome dash knobs were included, too. Sales of the classy CST models increased each year—12,588 hit the streets in 1967, followed by 16,755 the next year, and 29,942 in 1969.

The option was even offered for the heavy-duty Camper Special pickups, demonstrating that Chevy officials had indeed recognized a newfound need among the ever-growing recreational set to have their cake and eat it, too. Weekend wayfarers, vacationing vagabonds, restless

Above
Far less popular than the Blazer was another new 1969 model, the Longhorn. Featuring a stretched wheelbase and lengthened cargo box, the heavy-duty Longhorn was created with the growing hordes of campers in mind.

Left
The white needle on this 1968 C10's speedometer is part of the optional speed-warning system. The driver chose at what speed he wanted to hear the warning by turning the little knob at the upper left.

Above
If you can't beat 'em, join 'em. That's what Chevrolet officials did in 1972 when they turned to Japan to help them market the LUV compact pickup. The last LUV was sold in 1983 just as Chevy's own S-10 was debuting.

Far right
Many collectors today consider the last two pickups of the 1967-1972 run to be the best looking, thanks to their sporty grilles. Most sporty of all was the Super Cheyenne, introduced in 1972.

Far right inset
Chevrolet first offered the Cheyenne trim package in 1971, then followed it up with the Super Cheyenne option the following year. Once again, extra exterior trim and a jazzed-up interior was part of the plan.

retirees, and the rest apparently did want to see the U.S.A. in style *and* haul their camper or boat along for the ride. RV'ers continued fueling pickup demand during the late 1960s, and also helped boost V-8 sales along with other comfort and convenience options previously found mostly on the car side of the marketplace.

Following a 40-percent presence in 1966, V-8s found a place under 49 percent of Chevy truck hoods in 1967. That figure soared to 60.4 percent in 1968. Optional air conditioning grew more popular too, as did automatic transmissions. Chevrolet engineers had already proven that their three-speed Turbo-Hydra-Matic transmission was tough enough for truck duty by introducing it as a new option for hard-working three-quarter- and one-ton trucks in 1966. Automatics showed up on half of the annual truck production run by 1971, the same year Chevrolet made front disc brakes standard for the light-truck field. Truly un-truck-like features such as power door locks and a rear window defroster appeared as options in 1977.

The camping crowd was again the focus in 1969 when Chevrolet rolled out another new idea, this one named "Longhorn." Featuring a stretched 133-inch wheelbase and a lengthened 8.5-foot Fleetside cargo box, the Longhorn was able to handle the bulkiest and heaviest of slip-in truck campers. This truck came in three-quarter- and one-ton forms, and it too offered the various custom trim and comfort options. And like all of Chevy's heavier pickups and 4x4s, the Longhorn rode on leaf springs in back. As they had since 1963, half-tons that year continued using coil springs at both ends to offer pickup drivers at least some of the ride qualities commonly taken for granted by their automobile-owning brethren.

Not at all popular during its four-year run, the Longhorn was one of two specially targeted Chevy trucks to debut in 1969. The other remains famous to this day, and not just because it's still selling like nobody's business.

While most Blazer-driving soccer moms of the new millennium probably couldn't care less, the dependable,

The Super Cheyenne interior was easily the flashiest to that point in Chevy truck history.

all-purpose sport-utility vehicle that they've pledged their allegiance to will likely be mentioned someday among the truck market's various milestones. Right now the transformation of the modern transportation market is too fresh; history has yet to fully identify, let alone immortalize, those responsible for inducing the present parity between car and truck. But did the original Blazer play the biggest part?

Introduced midyear in 1969, Chevrolet's "little" SUV was basically a scaled-down rendition of the division's stylish, successful half-ton truck. Its attractive one-piece body rode on a shortened four-wheel-drive chassis suspended by leaf springs front and rear. The K5 Blazer's wheelbase was a scant 104 inches, compared to 115 for the conventional K10 Chevy pickup in 1969. Though the first K5 was nearly a foot shorter than its K10 cousin, it was still much bigger overall than the two off-road rivals that inspired its creation—International's Scout, born in 1961, and Ford's Bronco, created five years later. Like those two truly small 4x4s, the 1969 Blazer came standard in topless form to enhance its appeal as a fun, sun-loving machine. A removable fiberglass roof was optional.

Chevy engineers redesigned their 4x4 pickup platform in 1967 to bring down overall vehicle height without compromising clearance on the dirty side. They achieved this effect by attaching the transfer case directly to the transmission in a higher location than before, allowing a "shorter" suspension to take its place underneath. The distance between dirt and case remained 12.5 inches for the 1967 K10, but the truck's overall top-to-bottom measurement was five inches less than it had been in 1966. Diminishing that tall, hulking, top-heavy stance was Chevrolet's first real step towards merging its 4x4 family into the mainstream. Bringing out the K5 Blazer in 1969 was the second, and therein lies at least part of the reasoning behind its nomination to the utility-vehicle hall of fame.

Off-roading, of course, was nothing new when the Blazer first came around the bend. Willys (later reformed as Kaiser-Jeep) had been number one in this dusty field dating back to the end of World War II. And no, the K5 Chevy did not originate the SUV craze—Chevrolet's own Suburban dates back to 1935; International's Travelall appeared in 1956; and Kaiser-Jeep's Wagoneer rolled out in 1963. The 1969 Blazer, though clearly a potentially cool recreational cruiser, wasn't even the first

to abstractly pair "sport" with "utility." The 1961 Scout undoubtedly deserves that honor, then Ford made it official from a lexicon angle in 1966 by introducing the "Sports Utility" version of its new Bronco. So how did Chevrolet make truck history in 1969?

Basically the Blazer was the first to tie these trendy loose ends into one unified concept, a "best-of-both-worlds" school of thought that 30-some years later dominates Detroit. During the 1960s pickups proved they could step up as a "second car." By the 1990s next to no one was questioning the SUV's ability to replace the primary car. Easily representing one of the most significant steps during the SUV's early evolvement, the original Blazer laid the foundation for a bridge between car and truck worlds that stands stronger than ever today. And it did so in four-wheel-drive fashion, a style previously considered unfit for polite society.

Today's movers-and-shakers never think twice about driving a 4x4 or sport-ute everyday to work, to play, wherever. Refining the four-wheel-drive platform—making it easier to operate and own even for the meekest of car buyers—contributed greatly to the SUV's surge in popularity. But that refinement didn't

gain real momentum until recent decades. As late as the 1970s, the off-road market was still best left to adventurers, if not downright daredevils. Few took this segment seriously during the 1960s, even after Ford followed International's lead into the fun 4x4 field. Then General Motors showed up. "Ol' Number One is now involved, so there must be something to this four-wheel-drive, off-the-road epidemic," wrote Julian Schmidt in his April 1969 *Motor Trend* review of the new Chevy truck that meant different things to different drivers.

Though the diminutive duo from International and Ford were inherently more nimble, the multi-role 1969 Blazer could naturally haul considerably more of whatever you wanted to stuff in it. With the back seat removed and tailgate lowered, the bed floor measured eight feet long, amounting to as much practical utility as most typical pickups offered. With the back seat back in place, you could carry the dog and kids to the beach, all the way to water's edge if you wanted, thanks to the K5's ample off-road capabilities. As rugged and ready as any Chevy 4x4, the Blazer was nonetheless much easier to handle than its longer, heavier running mates under any

The optional sliding rear window on this 1973 half-ton represented additional proof of the importance of the camper crowd to Chevrolet sales experts in the 1960s and 1970s.

153

conditions, especially when fitted with all the car-like convenience options.

"Though longer and wider than competitive bob-tailed rigs, it's quite nimble in back country use and, with power steering and an automatic transmission, very easy to drive," wrote Ed Orr of *Speed Age*. "Here is a machine that performs credibly on the freeway, but its shine really comes through when the dust begins to fly."

Along with all that, the 1969 Blazer, like the pickup it was based on, looked great. According to Orr, it introduced "a new standard of style to the four-wheel-drive field." And again, like the pickup it sprung from, the Blazer could be made even more attractive with the CST package, which among other things included the removable fiberglass top.

A conventional two-wheel-drive Blazer debuted in 1970 to widen the appeal further (although few were sold each year before the 4x2 model was cancelled after 1983), and Chevrolet's first full-time four-wheel-drive setup appeared in 1974. Blazer popularity understandably stayed on the fast track throughout the decade. Following the 4,935 built in 1969, total production (both two- and four-wheel-drive) was 12,512 in 1970, 18,497 in 1971, and 47,623 in 1972. Sales then soared to 74,389 in 1976, followed by 90,987 in 1979.

As demand for the Blazer was first heating up in the early 1970s, Chevrolet planners decided to jump on another trendy bandwagon, this one featuring quite a different breed of utility vehicle. By 1971 sales of imported compact trucks, mostly Japanese, had risen to alarming levels, influencing Detroit to respond just as it had after Volkswagen had helped inspire the introduction of Ford's Econoline and Chevrolet's Corvair 95 trucks in 1961. If you can't beat 'em, join 'em apparently was the conclusion once again.

In March 1972 Chevrolet dealers began offering the Light Utility Vehicle, or "LUV" for short. Built by GM affiliate Isuzu Motors of Tokyo, the LUV was imported to America and badged as a Chevy product. This affordable mini-pickup's wheelbase was a tidy 102.4 inches, while its payload rating was 1,100 pounds. A heavy-duty frame, economical four-cylinder power, and nice-riding torsion-bar independent front suspension all worked in concert to make the LUV an able rival to all those Datsuns and Toyotas then flooding across the Pacific. Sold mostly in coastal regions early on, the first LUV found more than 21,000 buyers in 1972. Popularity then understandably increased as gasoline prices began to rise. Sales of LUVs surpassed 70,000 in 1978 then hit 100,000 the following year before demand began to wane. The fate of Chevrolet's first truly compact pickup was sealed in 1982 when GM began building its own mini-trucks. About 15,000 leftover '82 LUVs were sold in 1983 alongside Chevy's new S-10 . . . but that's another story for another chapter.

As for Chevrolet's conventional half-ton, its appeal was enhanced further on various occasions during the 1970s, most notably in 1973 when the light-truck line was refined yet again inside and out. An even roomier cab went on top of a beefed-up frame, and exterior styling was jazzed up once more. More class, more luxury, and more options were among the goals that year. More

and more sales resulted. In November 1973 Chevrolet beancounters announced that their half-ton Fleetside pickup had become General Motors' best-selling product, car or truck. This achievement was partially credited to a new class of truck buyers—most prominently women and city folk—who had discovered that a hard-working pickup could also be an attractive second vehicle.

Most attractive was the Cheyenne model, which first appeared in 1971 to pick up where the CST left off and raise the luxury ante higher than ever. Along with two-tone paint and eye-catching exterior trim, the Cheyenne package also dressed up the Chevy truck interior to the nines. "Deep-twist" carpeting, a custom steering wheel, plush vinyl upholstery with colorful cloth inserts, and a special headliner and door panel trim were just a few of the fancy features included. Bucket seats were also available on the popular Cheyenne. First-time sales in 1971 exploded to more than 72,000.

An even fancier Super Cheyenne option joined the Cheyenne within the year to make the Chevy truck more luxurious than many cars. Among the extra baubles and brightwork included in this deal were simulated woodgrain bodyside appliques—which could be had as an option on the regular Cheyenne pickup. Super Cheyenne interiors stood out with their hound's-tooth pattern seat inserts, one of various flashy cloth options offered to Chevy truck buyers beginning in the 1970s. Exterior paint choices blossomed too during the decade.

Chevy restructured its pickup line in 1975 to better identify a pecking order that grew increasingly more prestigious as a buyer scaled the price ladder. The base model was now the Custom Deluxe, followed by the trimmed-out Scottsdale, the cool Cheyenne, and a new flagship in place of the Super Cheyenne. Featuring all the bells and whistles, this top-shelf truck was given a name still familiar today: Silverado.

Various other pet names for special Chevy pickups have come and gone since the 1970s, but the title given to the best of the best has remained the same during all those years. Today Silverado still stands for a lot of truck—a tough, solid-as-a-rock machine made up of the most class, comfort, and convenience Chevrolet has ever offered to pickup buyers. Like Cal Ripken, Jr., the Silverado and its running mates simply won't quit, which helps explain why customers are still crazy for Chevy trucks some 80 years after the company first began building them.

Far left
Yet another restyle came in 1973 to further enhance the Chevy pickup's appeal. Late that year Chevrolet officials announced that their latest Fleetside pickup had become GM's best-selling product.

Far left inset
Custom Deluxe models were the next step up in prestige above the base Custom pickup in 1973. Further up the ladder were the Cheyenne and Super Cheyenne.

Epilogue
Chevy Pickups Just Keep on Truckin'

Above
Chevrolet introduced diesel power as a pickup option for the first time in 1978. Reportedly as much as 20 to 25 percent more fuel efficient than its gas-charged counterpart, the 5.7-liter (350-ci) V-8 diesel was rated at 120 horsepower in 1978.

Left
What a difference nearly half a century makes. A Chevy truck was truly a truck in 1946 (left); in 1990 the new SS 454 pickup was both a hot rod and a hard-working hauler.

How soon we forget. Not even a generation ago trucks were trucks and cars were cars. And that was that. Now we have pickups and automobiles playing together rather nicely on a level field, a situation that may have inspired more than one old-timer to wonder what possibly could come next. There's no way our parents could have predicted that the day would come when light trucks looked so damned good they'd be more popular than cars.

But here we are. Nowadays most Americans younger than 35 would never consider questioning the pickup's place in the everyday scheme of things. That light trucks, sport-utes, and other pickups can ably serve multi-purpose roles as both practical, purposeful transports and prestige-packed playthings has been a fully recognized reality for at least 10 years.

About a decade before that, Detroit planners recognized that they soon would be selling utility vehicles as fast as they could build them. As late as 1983, new cars were still outnumbering new trucks by a healthy 2:1 margin, but that ratio was nearly 7:1 just 20 years before. Production records in the truck field then fell repeatedly during the late 1980s after the utility vehicle's share of the transportation market surpassed 30 percent for the first time in 1985. Total truck sales hit the 5 million mark in 1987, and the market share continued to rise from there. It was 34.3 percent in 1990, 40-flat in 1993. A 50-50 split was in hand as the century wound down.

A nice combination of off-road toughness and around-town comfort, the ZR-2 package appeared for the S-10 pickup in 1994.

Light-truck popularity grew so prominent during the 1990s, GM officials found themselves faced with a new reality: It was time to pay Peter by robbing Paul. As Ford officials seemingly discovered first, runaway light-truck sales, spurred on primarily by the SUV, were deflating demand for various car models. Most affected was the two-door coupe, once a popular plaything for the young and young-at-heart. Ford's famous Thunderbird, seriously sagging in sales, was unceremoniously cancelled in 1997. Chevrolet officials waited a few years before confirming rumors that another legend would fall by the wayside, too, probably by the end of 2002. Yes, Virginia, the Camaro is history.

Ma and Pa never could have guessed that one either, and even some in the 35-and-under set find it hard to believe. Many car-lovers, old or young, may

The SS 454's big-block V-8—it's hiding somewhere beneath all that plumbing and hardware—was rated at 230 horsepower in 1990.

think it a crime, but we just can't argue with the numbers. Profit margins on trucks remain higher than those on cars, and the demand for more and more trucks shows no sign of reversing. GM's decision to cancel the slow-selling F-body coupe (Camaro/Firebird) was nothing personal, it was just business—good business.

Life in the truck business these days is fast-paced, to say the least. Resting on laurels is for losers, as all rivals can't seem to come out with the latest, greatest variation on the utility-vehicle theme quick enough. Without a doubt few truck buyers even five years later remembered that Chevy's C/K pickups were the first on the market with a "passenger-friendly" third-door option in 1996. Ford designers wasted little time rolling out a standard third door for their redesigned F-150 SuperCab in 1997, and four-door cabs were soon flooding the marketplace.

Chevrolet's redesigned Silverado pickup won *Motor Trend's* "Truck of the Year" trophy in 1999, but that didn't seem good enough in a marketplace dominated by the "what-have-you-done-for-me-lately" attitude of the consumers. Chevy revamped its truck line two years

later, resulting in yet another *Motor Trend* award, this time for the brutish, brawny Silverado Heavy Duty.

"The superlative power of our new heavy-duty Silverado and [GMC] Sierra, coupled with their best-in-class capabilities, durability and improved efficiency, nail every customer requirement and then some," said Tom Stephens,[AUTH: Stephens correct?] GM vice president and group director of the Pontiac Vehicle Engineering Center. "They provide customers with nothing less than a new standard for this segment."

Indeed, the big, beautiful 2001 Silverado HD trucks represented an all-new high in class, comfort, and convenience for the real men among truck buyers. No big pickups before (the HD line includes tough-as-nails three-quarter- and one-ton regular cabs, four-door cabs, and crew cabs) could work that hard while looking that good. Then again, name a Chevy truck that hasn't filled that bill over the last 40 years or so.

Style and class have been important priorities right along with durability and strength since the 1960s. Chevy pickups grew better looking each time pen went to paper; 1973's redesign was more attractive than 1967's,

Right
Chevrolet beat both Ford and Dodge to the punch with a true-blue American-made compact pickup with its first S-10 in late 1982.

Far right
A redesigned Blazer in 1995 featured four-wheel anti-lock brakes and a driver's side airbag.

which outdid 1960's. In 1981, a new aerodynamic nose was grafted onto the 1973 body; this new combination rolled on to 1987. Excess weight was also trimmed off in 1981 to further increase efficiency. GM then reportedly spent $1.3 billion to redesign the Chevy truck for 1988.

At the time, the all-new 1988 C/K truck stood as the most extensively tested vehicle ever created by General Motors. Interior ergonomics were investigated every bit as intently as aerodynamics, fuel efficiency. and overall performance. Among its notable innovations was its standard anti-lock rear brakes, another probably-forgotten first for a full-sized pickup. Further enhancements included an electronically controlled four-speed automatic transmission in 1993, two new 6.5-liter turbocharged diesel V-8s in 1994, and a driver's side airbag (for models less than 8,600 pounds) in 1995.

The familiar C/K model designations were overshadowed when the redesigned Silverado made the scene in 1999, basically because Chevy officials wanted their latest new truck to be best known by a suitably attractive

name. "Silverado is the epitome of the Chevy truck brand image," said Chevrolet General Mmanager John Middlebrook in 1998. "It takes quality, dependability, performance and comfort to a whole new level." The latest Silverado continues raising the bar.

Present-day 4x4 buyers probably also don't recall that Chevrolet helped popularize full-time four-wheel-drive, an advancement that allowed off-road vehicles easier acceptance onto Mainstreet U.S.A. Chevrolet was also the first to offer a compact SUV, this coming in 1983. At the time, saving bucks, both at the gas pump and on your friendly neighborhood dealer's lot, was still very much job one around Detroit. Various concessions to the fuel crunch in previous years included the imported LUV mini-pickup in the 1970s and optional diesel power for Chevrolet's conventional truck line in 1978.

A Chevy-designed and -built compact, the S-10, then debuted for 1982 about six months before Ford and Dodge rolled out their first Ranger and Rampage, respectively. One year later a smaller, more affordable

Above
Even in its last model year, the 19'98 C/K truck was by no means old news. This Z71 K1500 features most of the comforts of home, including a third door on the passenger side. Chevrolet was the first to offer an optional third door in 1996.

Right
Chevrolet's redesigned Silverado truck was *Motor Trend's* "Truck of the Year" in 1999. *Motor Trend* Publisher Doug Hamlin (second from left) hands over the award to Chevrolet General Manager John Middlebrook. To the right is GM Vice President Michael Grimaldi; to the left is Silverado Brand Manager Kurt Ritter.

Blazer, based on the S-10 chassis, was introduced to once again get the competitive juices flowing; then Ford's Ranger-based Bronco II sport-ute showed up in 1984. Like the full-sized T-10 Blazer, its S-10 running mate was built only in two-door fashion at first. Four-door Blazers appeared midyear in 1990 as 1991 models, signaling further expansion of the SUV field.

Like their pickup running mates, Chevrolet's sport-utilities are now available in a wide array of sizes with two or four doors. The ever-present Suburban (available only as a four-door) still leads the way in both price and size, while the Blazer brings up the bottom end. In between, the Tahoe fills the notch formerly occupied by the "big" K-series Blazer. After the full-sized Tahoe appeared in 1995 as a "shortened Suburban," the Blazer name was left solely to the compact crowd. An upscale four-door "TrailBlazer" model was introduced in 1999 after Chevrolet product planners detected a difference between two- and four-door SUV customers.

"Two-door buyers are more likely to go off-road," explained Blazer Brand Manager Russ Clark. "Four-door buyers want the attributes of a truck, with a very refined, distinctive appearance—just like TrailBlazer."

Two years after its introduction, the four-door TrailBlazer was reborn on a new GM platform (shared with the GMC Envoy and Oldsmobile Bravada) featuring, among other things, an innovative "hydroformed" frame. Hyrdroforming uses some serious water pressure to forcibly shape and bend steel tubing, resulting in one-piece frame rails that offer more strength with less mass than their welded-up forerunners. The C5 Corvette was first to demonstrate this process in 1997.

The idea behind the redesigned TrailBlazer was to match rivals in yet another expanding SUV niche. "What we want people to realize is that the Blazer is not going away, and the TrailBlazer is a completely new vehicle which will compete in the midsize SUV market," added Clark in 2001. "Blazer invented the compact utility segment in 1983, but the 2002 TrailBlazer will redefine the existing midsize utility market. It will allow our buyers to go beyond everyday life because TrailBlazer sets new standards for what an SUV should be."

Chevrolet pushed the outside of the envelope even further in 2001 with its totally fresh Avalanche, first

shown in concept form at the North American Auto Show in Detroit in January 2000. According to Chevrolet General Manager Kurt Ritter, the Avalanche "represents the creation of an entirely new 'ultimate utility vehicle' segment. [It] combines the roominess of Suburban-style first- and second-row seating with the practicality of a Silverado-style cargo box. It can be reconfigured to function as either a pickup or an SUV or both at the same time."

As Avalanche ads explained in 2001, "it adapts, but it never conforms." Just when truck buyers thought they'd seen it all, along comes a split-personality vehicle that somehow covers all bases at once. Chevrolet designers accomplished this feat by creating their "Convert-a-Cab" system with its unique "midgate" partition. Transforming the comfortable four-door Avalanche into a full-sized cargo-carrying pickup is as simple as folding up the 60-40 passenger seat, folding down the midgate, and removing the cab's rear window—it stores on the midgate. All this folding

The Vortec family of truck engines seemingly improved every year during the 1990s. The Vortec V-8 for 1999 was still running as big as 454 cubic inches (7.4 liters). Top Vortec output was 290 horsepower.

Next pages
Most reports claim the exciting SSR pickup will differ little from this concept vehicle when it goes into production late in 2002. Whatever changes are made, it will still be the coolest Chevy truck yet to cruise the boulevard.

The Silverado Heavy Duty line picked up *Motor Trend's* Truck of the Year honors in 2001.

results in an extended pickup bed floor that measures eight-feet, one-inch long, compared to five-foot-three in the standard SUV mode. What will they think of next? How 'bout a hot rod truck?

As this epic goes to press, Chevrolet's quick-thinking truck guys are busy preparing yet another "ultimate utility vehicle." No, the Super Sports Roadster (SSR) won't be Detroit's first hot-to-trot pickup when it goes into production late in 2002. Among others, GMC's sizzling Syclone and Chevy's big, bad, and black SS 454, both introduced in the early 1990s, certainly qualified as super-cool cargo carriers with playful natures. But there's no mistaking where the SSR's inspiration came from, and there's no doubting how much excitement it will inspire.

"People from 6 to 60 will turn their heads when SSR comes down the street, just as they did with the 1957 Chevy Bel Air, the 1963 Corvette String Ray, and the Chevelle SS 396," said Kurt Ritter.

The overall look is retro all the way, inspiring remembrances of both vintage Chevy pickups and classic street rods of the 1930s and 1940s. But the feel behind the wheel is totally now. The SSR brings back fond memories of days gone by while toying with the imagination of its driver with a decent dose of modern technology. GM CEO Richard Wagoner, Jr., called it "a unique combination of many characteristics—a sportscar, pickup and roadster—in one striking package." "No other manufacturer has a vehicle like SSR,"

added Ritter. "No one has this much fun and function in one package."

First unveiled to the public in concept-vehicle form at the Detroit Auto Show in January 2000, the SSR will roll literally unchanged from the rotating stage to the street. That retractable hardtop, rear-driven V-8 drivetrain, and sporty chassis (based loosely on the new TrailBlazer's hydroformed foundation) will carry over. Five-spoke alloy sport wheels wearing huge treads (19-inch fronts, 20-inch rears) will hold things up, and an all-aluminum Vortec 5300 Gen III small-block putting out nearly 300 horses will get things going. There won't be any cargo capacity to speak of, but there will be tons of cool.

"You drive some vehicles because you have to," said Ed Welburn, director of the GM Corporate Brand Character Center. "But you drive this vehicle because you want to."

Why GM officials opted to put this flight of fancy into regular production is a good question, especially considering the then-current tough economic times around Detroit and the rest of the country. Clearly some inspiration came from Ford's Thunderbird and Chrysler's PT Cruiser, and some critics have gone as far as to claim that the SSR, to some degree, represents compensation for killing the Camaro. Whatever the reasons, this playful pickup will certainly be a joy to drive—as much as any car out there. And like all other Chevy trucks down through time, it will be solid. Kinda like a rock.

A redesigned TrailBlazer appeared in 2002 to help Chevrolet saturate the SUV market with entries at all size levels.

Index

American Bantam, 42
Autocar, 23
Automotive Industries, 20
Big Three, 42–45, 60, 89
Blue Oval Boys, 20
Bright, Jim, 48
Chevrolet Motor Company, 17, 35, 47
Chevrolet, Louis, 17
Chrysler Corporation, 42
Cole, Ed, 74, 76
Crapo, William, 17
Datsun, 24
Dearborn, 35, 39, 48
Diamond T, 43
Dodge, 24, 25, 42
Dodge, Horace, 33
Dodge, John, 33
Dunlop, John, 27,
Durant, Billy, 17, 19, 20
Eisenhower, Dwight, 29
Federal Highway Act of 1921, 29
Federal, 42
Fish, William, 74
Fisher Body Corporation, 3, 55
Ford, 42, 43, 47–49, 73
Ford, Henry, 17, 23, 25, 29, 32, 35–37, 39, 41, 45, 47, 73
General Motors, 17, 48
Graham Brothers, 25, 33
Hercules, 40, 41
Hudson, 52, 53, 60, 61
IFS construction, 130
International Harvester, 42, 49, 63
Interstate Highway Act, 29
Jordan, Chuck, 76, 87
Keating, Thomas, 74
Knox, 27
Knudsen, William S., 37, 39, 41
Mack, 42, 43

Martin-Parry, 35, 40, 41
Melton, Harold, 69
Models
  3100 series, 126
  3200 series, 126
  3600 series, 126
  3800 series, 126
  Advance Design pickups, 57–71, 74, 87
  Apache, 126
  Blazer, 49, 154, 155
  Bronco, 49
  C "conventional truck, 126
  C/K pickups, 126
  C20 V-8 pickup, 125
  Cameo Carrier, 88–91, 125
  Carryall Suburban, 49
  Chevy's little big rig, 68, 69
  Corvair 95 pickups, 131–141, 155
  Coupe Pickups, 52, 53
  Custom Sport Truck, (CST), 149, 155
  El Camino, 102–117
  FA-series, 22
  Four wheel drive pickups, 78, 79
  Hot One, 74, 75
  K "four-wheel drive, 126
  K10 pickup, 152
  L "low cab forward", 126
  Loadmaster, 60–71, 87
  Longhorn, 150, 151
  M "tandem-axles, 126
  Master 85, 53
  Model 10, 43
  Model 201, 43
  Model 222, 43
  Model 490, 18, 21, 30, 31, 36,126
  Model 80, 43
  Model A, 37, 39, 41
  Model ED, 43

Model G, 31
Model T, 36, 37, 39–41
Model TT, 24, 29, 30, 33, 55
P "forward control", 126
Power Wagon, 78
Ranchero, 106–117
RPO Z81, the Camper Special deal, 125
S "school bus", 126
SS 454, 166
Screenside, 25
Silverado, 159
Spartan, 126
Speedwagon, 29
Suburban, 48, 49, 152
Task Force trucks, 85–91, 129, 145, 146
Thriftmaster, 60–71, 87
Viking, 127
Moreland, 42
Mustang Trailer, 68, 69
NAPCO, 78, 79, 87
Olds, Ransom E., 42
Olson, Albert Jr., 107
Packard, 60
Phillips, Bob, 76
Plymouth, 52, 53, 73
Relay, 42
REO, 42, 43
Rugby, 42
Schact, 42
Sloan, Alfred Jr., 19, 20
Studebaker, 43, 52, 60, 89, 103,104
The Depression, 40, 42
Wells, David, 23
White, 23
Woods, John, 58
World War II, 43, 52–55, 57, 62